THE MAN WHO WAS Q
The True Story of Charles Fraser-Smith, the 'Q' Wizard of World War II

Books by Charles Fraser-Smith

The Secret War of Charles Fraser-Smith.	(£3.50. p & p 80p)
Secret Warriors.	(£2.50. p & p 80p)
Men of Faith in World War II.	(£2.50. p & p 80p)
Four Thousand Year War.	(£3.20. p & p 80p)
The Man Who was 'Q' (by David Porter)	(£3.95. p & p 80p)

Obtainable, autographed, from:

**MRS. M. S. FRASER-SMITH
LITTLE COMPASS
1 WESTGATE
LOUTH
LINCOLNSHIRE
LN11 9YN**

The most complete collection of secret gadgets in Britain, as described in Charles Fraser-Smith's books, is on display at Bickleigh Castle, Nr. Tiverton, Devon. Open Easter to end of May – Wednesdays, Sundays and Bank Holidays. June to mid-October daily (except Saturdays) 2 to 5 p.m. Parties by arrangement. Telephone: 0884 855363. Also at Dover Castle, Dover, Kent. Open Daily, closed 24–26 December and 1st January.

The Man Who Was Q

The True Story of Charles Fraser—Smith, the 'Q' Wizard of World War II

DAVID PORTER

M. S. FRASER-SMITH

Cover design by Design Works

Pictures: (xiv) Fritz Curzon,
Norwich NR16 1RW

(xxi) (xxii) Tony Freeman
Press Agency, Barnstaple

British Library Cataloguing in Publication Data

Porter, David, *1945–*
   The man who was Q.
   1. Christian Church. Evangelism. Fraser-Smith, Charles,
   1904–1992
   I. Title
   269'.2'0924

   ISBN 0–85364–481–0

Typeset by Photoprint, Torquay, Devon
and Printed in Great Britain for M. S. Fraser-Smith,
by Cox & Wyman Ltd., Reading.

CONTENTS

INTRODUCTORY NOTE
By David Porter

In working with Charles Fraser-Smith on his life-story, I have been given full access to his notes and papers, and both Charles and Lin have given me any information I have asked for. I have been given hospitality both at Charles and Lin's home, and also by Brian Fraser-Smith who answered my questions about farming methods and showed me round the family farm. And I am grateful to a number of other people who have given me additional recollections and opinions, and to my publishers Paternoster Press.

A biography of a living person, written as this has been with close collaboration between the author and his subject, will necessarily contain the opinions of both. It should be clear from context when a particular statement originates from Charles or myself. In addition, the source for much of the information contained in this book is Charles Fraser-Smith himself, though other sources have been used where available. Generally speaking, Charles's own personal records and notes have been used as the final arbiter where conflicting versions of events exist. I hope that this book will be of interest to all who have enjoyed Charles's books, and that it will introduce him to many who have yet to make his acquaintance.

CHAPTER ONE
Beginnings

Turkey calling . . . Turkey calling . . . Italy declares war on Britain and France . . . Turkey calling . . .

The broadcaster's voice was sombre; the news was grim. The Englishman seated by the wireless listened intently, his face thoughtful. He was in his mid-thirties, with a moustache and trim auburn hair. While he listened, he flicked irritably through papers on his desk, as if he could not bear to be idle for a moment, even while hearing news of a declaration of war on his homeland.

The terse bulletin came to an end. The solitary listener reached up, switched the radio off, and remained seated for a while. The noisy bustle of a Moroccan morning filtered through the open window. Eventually he reached for the telephone.

'Fraser-Smith here – have you heard the news?'

At the other end of the line, the staff of the French Government HQ in Morocco reacted in incredulity. Turkish Radio, as often happened, had managed to break a major world news story several hours before their French and British counterparts.

'Ring Paris,' he said brusquely. 'Get them to confirm it.' He rang off, and waited.

A few minutes later HQ called back. 'Paris confirms. Many thanks for telling us so quickly.'

Charles Fraser-Smith nodded an unseen acknowledgement. His cool, grey eyes narrowed. He replaced the receiver. There was a great deal to be organised.

Italy's declaration of war on June 10th, 1940, was greeted with international dismay. In London, the Lord Privy Seal, Clement Attlee, made a statement in Parliament:

> Hardly ever before in history can the decision to embroil a great nation in war have been taken so wantonly and with so little excuse . . .. Signor Mussolini has made a profound mistake.

On 14th June, Paris fell to the German forces. Four days later Winston Churchill addressed the House of Commons.

> What General Weygand called the 'Battle of France' is over. I expect that the battle of Britain is about to begin. Upon this battle depends the survival of Christian civilisation . . .. Let us therefore brace ourselves to our duty and so bear ourselves that if the British Commonwealth and Empire lasts for a thousand years men will still say, 'This was their finest hour.'

On 25th June, France surrendered, and Charles Fraser-Smith began to think about returning to England.

He had been in Morocco since 1926 when he was twenty-two years old, but even before then his career had been varied.

He was brought up in a Christian home at Croxley Green in Hertfordshire. It was an area full of interest to a young boy. One of the nearby families was the Tussaud family, of the famous Waxworks Museum. During the First World War, one of the Tussaud sons flew low over the Fraser-Smith's house and saw them having a meal on the terrace. He banked, dropped very low and flew back waving to them. It was a wonderful thrill which Charles remembered for the rest of his life.

Charles was educated at Watford Grammar School and

later at Brighton College, where he showed little academic promise. However, he was gifted in a variety of practical areas – science (especially electricity and magnetism), woodwork, and model-making; all skills which were to play a prominent part in his later life. He was also the youngest boy in the school ever to win a rugby cap.

His brother, Alfred, was of a more scientific turn of mind and eventually became a doctor. When Alfred was sixteen, he was invited to attend a Crusader camp by A.K. Kestin, the founder of the movement. The Crusaders, which are still very active today, ran Bible classes, camps and other activities (in those days, for boys only).

After the camp, Alfred went on to the family summer holiday by the sea at Littlehampton. He immediately started to organise boys' hockey matches on the beach, and in the evenings invited boys to the house to sing choruses. Soon the sing-songs had expanded to include reading a Bible passage, and a short talk from his aunt, Edith Piper, who was an able speaker. It was during that fortnight that Charles committed his life to Christ, and the beginnings of his call to the mission field began.[1]

On leaving Brighton College at the age of seventeen, Charles went to teach at a preparatory school near Portsmouth. There he coached the sons of naval officers in rugby, hockey and cricket. He also taught elementary science; giving photography lessons, wiring the buildings with electric bells, and at one point demonstrating simple explosive theory with home-made guns made from strong metal tubing and gunpowder (the latter activity was stopped by the authorities, being considered too dangerous even for the sons of naval officers).

He also started a Crusader Class at the school. So the two later enthusiasms of his life – Bible teaching and mechanical ingenuity – were apparent even in his late teens.

The Portsmouth post was for a year. Frank and Edith Piper, the uncle and aunt who brought up the four Fraser-Smith children, intended him to go on to join his brother as a medical student at St Bartholomew's Hospital in London, but the plan came to nothing when Charles turned out to have a severe dislike of the sight of blood. His guardians next thought of engineering as a career for their nephew, and arranged for him to be interviewed by a Mr Hunter, who had been responsible for building the naval dockyard at Gibraltar.

It had been Mr Hunter, in his role as an elder at Cholmeley Hall (today renamed Cholmeley Evangelical Church), who had interviewed Charles when he was sixteen and a candidate for baptism by immersion. So the conversation about engineering was relaxed and cordial, but Charles disliked the prospect of the mathematical work involved as much as he had disliked the sight of blood. He did not become an engineer.

Instead he went to Littlehampton for three years to study farming with a Mr Vinnicombe. His guardians disapproved, but Charles persuaded them to let him go.

It turned out to be a crucial time. Again, Charles started a Crusader class in a local prep school. His interest in Bible teaching was crystallising.

And he was thinking hard about what he should be doing with his life. More importantly, what did God want him to be doing with it? If he was to be a farmer, whereabouts? Gradually his thoughts began to focus on missionary work, and a number of circumstances seemed to point to Morocco.

One of these circumstances was his family background. The four children were orphaned when Charles was seven years old, and the Pipers adopted them. Charles's father, who was a solicitor and also owned a wholesale grocery business, had died at the early age of thirty-three. He and his wife had been nominally Church of England, but the family did not attend church regularly.

By contrast, the Pipers were keen Christians. Charles's uncle had a Church of England background, and his aunt an Open Brethren background. They attended the Croxley Green Brethren Church, though his uncle preached occasionally at local Methodist and Baptist churches. The childrens' governess was from the Church of England, and they were often taken to the local parish church, and frequently the whole family went to wherever Charles's uncle was preaching. And in the holidays, there were a number of interdenominational activities such as Crusaders and Children's Special Service Mission.

So Charles was fortunate; he grew up without a tenacious attachment to a particular denomination. On the whole he preferred the Open Brethren pattern of worship, though in those days it was not worship which offered a great deal to children (of the Exclusive, or Closed Brethren, he knew nothing at all.) He was brought up in the tradition of family prayers. After breakfast in the house at Croxley Green, all work ceased; and family, maids and gardener (for whom a pair of slippers was provided for the occasion!) gathered in the study for prayer, when various missionaries were prayed for regularly and fervently. On the study wall was a framed photograph of Robert Cleaver Chapman, a well-known figure in missionary work in Spain, who became a hero to the young Charles.

Edith Piper (then "Smith") had felt called to go to Spain in the early 1900s to work with the Children's Special Service Mission, which later became the Scripture Union. She went to Barnstaple in Devon (where Charles himself was to settle in 1963), to seek the advice of Robert Chapman. He gave his blessing to her plans, and as she prepared to go home, he began to pray for her safety.

The cab arrived to take her to the station, but Chapman was still praying. She did not dare to interrupt, and the cab had to wait until the prayer came to an end. She missed the train as a result. A few hours later she heard the news that the same train had been involved in a horrendous accident. Convinced that God had protected her for a purpose, she went to Spain and was a missionary for several years.

Through her influence, her two sisters trained as missionary nurses. One went to Spain, the other to Tangier. The former, before her twenty-fifth birthday, translated the Daily Light Bible reading notes into Spanish, and passages of Scripture into Braille for the Spanish blind community. The latter translated Mark's Gospel into colloquial Arabic before she was twenty-six years old; she died in a typhoid epidemic at the age of twenty-seven, and her younger sister went to Tangier to take her place, dying herself at the age of twenty-six.

Both sisters were on the staff of the North Africa Mission, and Edith Smith, after she returned from the mission field and married Frank Piper in 1910, retained a close interest in the Mission's activities. She knew its founder, Mr E. Glenny, and its Honorary Secretary, Colonel George Wingate, the father of the famous Chindit leader General Orde Wingate;[2] and when Charles began to show a serious interest in North Africa, she arranged for the Director of the North Africa Mission, Dr Farmer, to meet him.

Charles explained his growing conviction that he should go to Morocco as a missionary and, like the apostle Paul before him, support himself by a trade, in his case agriculture. Dr Farmer listened sympathetically. An association with the North Africa Mission began then which was to last for the whole of Charles's life.

But missionary work of the kind that Charles had outlined was in those days unacceptable to the North Africa Mission, or indeed to any missionary society. So when he went to Morocco, he went as a pioneering 'non-professional missionary'. After the Second World War, this method became known as 'industrial missionary work', and today such workers are known as 'tent-makers', after the apostle Paul who earned his living by making tents.

Still anxious to test his new vocation, Charles began to put money aside, and eventually had enough saved to be able to go to Morocco for a tantalisingly brief tourist holiday. He spent most of his time in the Tangier zone, where he visited various missionary centres; an orphanage, a North Africa Mission hospital, and others.

He came back convinced that God wanted him in Morocco. The decision made, with characteristically meticulous precision he drew up a training timetable. First he completed his apprenticeship with Mr Vinnicombe, and left in 1925 with a good grasp of basic farming skills.

His next step was to become fluent in French, the main 'European' language of Morocco. He applied for, and was awarded, a place at the Institute Biblique in Paris.

He spent an invaluable year in France, which prepared him in many ways for life in the French Protectorate of Morocco. Charles's sister also stayed for a time in Paris, at the home of a family friend, Admiral Dalencourt, who gave Charles a motto which he never forgot: *Sans Dieu – rien* (Without God – nothing).

A friendship with a young Belgian Methodist led to the formation of a Parisian rugby team. Today France is a great rugby nation, but in the 1920s the game was virtually unknown, and matches were frequently held up by lengthy disputes about the rules.

Charles sampled the local Brethren church, and found the services not to his liking, but picked up some useful advice from the Brethren concerning French restaurants: never order casserole, mince, or mashed potatoes, for all of them can be resurrected from previous diners' leftovers. Charles followed the advice conscientiously.

He attempted to start a Paris Crusader class, but eventually had to abandon the project because of lack of support. With the help of a young English schoolmaster he did manage to start a small Bible study group, though he was not in Paris long enough to see it properly established.

Charles did not spend all his time in Paris. He spent part of the year in the south of France, where he stayed with a Mr and Mrs Arnera near Marseilles. Mr Arnera had a motorised caravan of the Open Air Mission for evangelistic work in the towns and villages around the region. In August, while he was staying there, an Italian Christian joined them. He was a successful electrical engineer who had disagreed violently with Mussolini's policies and had been forced to flee the country in his yacht. He mentioned to Charles that the lira had been massively devalued, and that six or seven pounds sterling would buy enough Italian money to stay in Italy for a month. Furthermore, he added, he had been responsible for the wiring of a new Salvation Army hostel in Rome. It was not yet open, but if Charles were to mention his new friend's name to the wardens, he would certainly be allowed to stay there for twopence a night.

It was too good an opportunity to let slip. Next day, Charles left for Rome.

It was not his first expedition abroad, but it was a profoundly important one in his developing plans. He was made welcome in Rome by the Salvation Army wardens, and after a meal was soon answering perceptive and sympathetic questions about his call to missionary work and the pioneering work he was hoping to do. He responded warmly to their interest.

They presented him with a key to the building and told him he was free to come and go as he pleased. Fascinated by the ancient city, he visited over twenty churches, and was both enthralled and appalled by what he saw. He wandered with other tourists in the Catacombs, and his imagination was seized by the ancient fonts for baptism by immersion, Christian inscriptions and other reminders of the early church. In the modern churches, however, he was confronted by a panoply of religious relics, ornaments and ritual which he found deeply offensive. His upbringing and natural inclination to simplicity and directness revolted at what he saw. The experience certainly profoundly affected his later Christian views and practice.

It was a glorious Italian summer. Charles travelled light; he managed with only two shirts, and the currency crisis worked decidedly in his favour. Bread and peaches

were ludicrously cheap, and one of Mussolini's innovations was a student rail ticket, covering the whole of Italy,
which cost the equivalent of ten shillings. He generally
travelled at night to save hotel bills, and a shirt rinsed out
in the train wash-basin dried in an hour. He visited
Florence, Venice, and Genoa, often travelling with young
Italian army officers who were also taking advantage of
Mussolini's train concessions.

It was a golden August, and a golden opportunity, and
Charles knew it. On one occasion he chatted to an Oxford
don who was scrutinising the reliefs on a triumphal arch
in Rome.

'This is an expensive city,' remarked the professor. 'I'm
paying 100 lire a day.'

Charles refrained from telling him that he himself was
paying one lira a day accommodation, and the princely
sum of another lira for each day's food.

Back in the South of France, he discovered that it was
possible to take the Moroccan driving examination in
Marseilles, and he signed up for a concentrated course, to
be examined on his last day in France. He arrived for the
test with his luggage packed, and after he had been
examined and awarded his driving brevet for the French
Protectorate of Morocco, the instructor drove him to the
station where he just managed to catch the Paris express.
The train arrived ten minutes late in Paris, jeopardising
an already precariously short connection which involved
crossing the city. Charles leaped into a taxi.

'Can one get to the Gare du Nord in time to catch the
London Express? It leaves in fifteen minutes!'

The cab driver shrugged phlegmatically. 'Possibly,
M'sieur, possibly . . .'

He slid into the traffic stream with an adroit clash of
gears, and hurtled towards the Gare du Nord. Soon,
however, a traffic jam confronted them, and Charles's
heart sank. The driver grinned, swerved onto the pave-
ment, and continued without loss of speed. He arrived at
the station with seconds to spare, received a large tip from

Charles, and departed in good humour while Charles caught his train. Within a few hours he was back in England.

Among the many new friends Charles had made at the Institute Biblique was a Scot, Bryce Nairn, who was also there to learn French. He planned to join his father, Cuthbert Nairn, who was Field Director of the Southern Moroccan Mission based in Marrakech and was later to die as a martyr at the hands of a Moroccan Arab in 1944.

Meeting Bryce Nairn was like finding the final piece of a jigsaw. He was a trained veterinary surgeon, and his father had been a farmer before going to Morocco. It was not long before Charles and Bryce were deep in plans to join forces; they would go out to Morocco together, buy farmland, and become pioneering missionaries.

There were long discussions and last-minute preparations. Necessities had to be bought, affairs tidied up in England, and family farewells said. But eventually everything was ready. In late Autumn, 1926, Charles and Bryce left England and arrived in Marrakech.

For the young Fraser-Smith, arriving in Morocco in 1926, the spell of the country was potent, and the first sight of the oasis of Marrakech, glimpsed from the Jibilat Hills thirty kilometres away, was magical. The venerable walls and buildings were surrounded by thousands of palm trees, and to the south the Atlas Mountains stretched away into the distance, their snow-tipped peaks suffused in a pink glow echoing the deep rose glow of the city walls. Winston Churchill persuaded Theodore Roosevelt to visit Marrakech with him after the Casablanca Conference of 1943. It was, he told Roosevelt, the most beautiful place in the world; and Charles Fraser-Smith, the young missionary whose later career was to bring him into the worlds of both those famous leaders, would not have disagreed with him.

CHAPTER TWO

Farming – Marrakech
and the Atlas Mountains

The ancients called Morocco *Il' Mogareb* – 'The Farthest-West Land', or 'The Land of the Setting Sun'. In those days it must have seemed so; it lay to the extreme west of their world, and beyond it stretched the endless unknown. For Charles Fraser-Smith and Bryce Nairn it was certainly a remote outpost, a place where the Christian gospel had made few inroads into the Muslim culture and where there was pioneering work to be done for God.

They stayed with Bryce's father in Marrakech, but it was not a time for relaxing. Cuthbert Nairn drilled them both in the rudiments of the Arabic language in every spare minute, and organised a rigorous study schedule for them. As the autumn turned to winter and the weather became chilly, the two sat at a table, their books spread out between them on a long table-cloth which draped over the table and almost touched the floor. Under the table was a charcoal brazier, which was changed regularly and provided welcome warmth for the students.

In breaks between studying, Charles renewed his acquaintance with the city of Marrakech. Much of the city – even today – is a mass of winding streets, full of alluring sights, sounds and smells; a street map resembles nothing so much as a sack of tangled eels. Charles browsed in the market stalls which spilled onto the street, and gazed at blank walls and large locked doorways in the walls hiding exotic palaces.

The centre of Marrakech life was a large open square,

an expanse of several acres, known as the Djemma el Fina. Storytellers, snake-charmers, conjurors, acrobats, sword-swallowers and scores of other entertainers performed there, each competing for the notice of the huge crowds that gathered there all day.

You could have your fortune told in the Djemma; if impotence was your problem, you could buy a potion to cure yourself; and if watching the dancers leaping with a snapping of castanets and wild rolling eyes made you thirsty, you could buy a drink from one of the numerous water-carriers. They strolled among the performers and their audiences, tinkling their small brass cups and touting for custom with words familiar from the Old Testament book of Isaiah: 'Ho, everyone who thirsts – here is water!'

Charles was often drawn to the Djemma. He was fascinated by the richness of life there. But the cacophony of performers shouting at the tops of their voices and the ceaseless patter of drums was too much for a European to bear for long, and he soon discovered a more peaceful place to relax: the garden adjoining the 200-foot tower of the Koutabia, one of many beautiful buildings left by the religious reformers and militant Muslims who had once been feared by all Europe as the Almohads. They conquered Spain and built a similar tower in Seville in AD 711. They planned to build towers in Paris and London, but were driven out of France at Tours in AD 732 by Charles Martel and finally expelled from Spain in AD 1212.

While he lived in the Marrakech area Charles was often to be seen in the Koutabia garden in his time off, especially in the hot months; sitting under an olive tree with the clamour of the Djemma a confused murmur in the distance, talking with Muslim friends. At moments like that, it was not difficult to think oneself back to biblical times. Jesus must often have sat under an olive tree, an oasis of peace in another oriental city, and gazed up at just such skies; empty, clear, and cool, translucent blue.

Charles and Bryce were not in Marrakech as sightseers. They had a vision which they longed to see fulfilled. They did not have to wait for long. After five months they were able to buy 250 acres of land lying halfway between Marrakech and the Atlas Mountains. The area was known as Tabahounite, so they called their place Tabahounite Farm.

Their ingenuity was put to the test immediately. An efficient irrigation system was an urgent need, and Bryce and Charles used a method that was then virtually unique to that area and to one place in the Sahara. It consisted of an underground tunnel system penetrating the gravel water table and feeding a large reservoir. The water table was about six metres below the surface, and was maintained in the summer by the melting snows on the Atlas Mountains, which are 12,300 feet high at their peak.

The cost in labour was considerable, and only 80 acres could be irrigated that way. The rest of the land was given over to grain crops and an olive grove, and was dependent on rain and on traditional methods of irrigation which had been practised as far back as biblical times. The results were variable at best.

The area that had been specially irrigated was very fruitful. Oranges, grapefruit, lemons, peaches, tomatoes, aubergines and many more crops were grown successfully, and produce was sold in Marrakech.

The whole enterprise was self-sufficient. Home-grown hemp provided all the ropes they needed; cattle produced milk, butter and cream; other livestock provided fresh meat. Fresh olives from the farm were a cheap luxury, and when added to meat provided the local *tajjin* dish, a delicious blend of sweet and savoury flavours. The oil from the olives was used for cooking, and when used in baking produced the finest pastry that Charles had ever tasted.

But though few British restaurants could have matched the quality of the food, Charles and Bryce were in little danger of forgetting that they were in a frontier situation in Marrakech. The world of Islam was all around them: the mosques, the ritual prayers, the voices from the high towers calling the faithful to worship, the elaborate, rich and colourful imagery of Muslim art and music.

On the farm, they had ample opportunity to encounter Islamic beliefs, often of a very primitive kind, as they worked side by side with local people whom they employed. For example, they had two house-boys; one was their cook, the other a cleaner. They slept in a room next to the kitchen. One morning, they came to Charles in great distress.

'We cannot stay any more. We go today. Now, at once.'

He raised his eyebrows. 'Why? What has happened, have we done something wrong? Is the work too hard? Perhaps you are lazy boys, perhaps I should find good workers?'

But they resisted his attempts to tease them back into good humour. Something was obviously frightening them. Charles became very concerned.

'Tell me what has happened. I will put it right. I will look after you.'

They shook their heads vigorously. 'Is no good. We go, we leave today, we finish.'

'I must know why,' he insisted. 'If something is wrong, you must tell me. Others might be frightened too. I will not allow you to leave until you tell me why you must leave.'

Eventually they gave in. The cook took a deep breath. 'In your well,' he stammered. His eyes rolled, and he was still trembling.

'What is in the well? Is it poisoned?'

'A *djin*, you have a *djin* in your well. There is an evil spirit in the water, we have heard it.'

Charles sighed. A reflection, probably, or a twig fallen in the water. It needed to be sorted out, whatever it was; the well supplying the house was a separate one, designed to ensure that the domestic water would be free from contamination. 'Fetch Mr Bryce,' he ordered.

Bryce arrived, and the little party went to the well, taking a strong rope with them. Bryce acted as anchor while Charles was lowered into the murky depths. The two boys stood petrified, expecting to see their master brought up as a dismembered corpse.

There was a long pause, punctuated only by a brief splashing, a chorus of groans from the boys, and a few muffled grunts from Charles. Then Bryce began hauling on the rope. Soon Charles reappeared, smiling and alive. He extended his clasped hands to the boys, who backed away in terror.

'Here, see; I have your *djin* in my hands, I have conquered it. Look. Don't be afraid.'

As the boys approached nervously, he opened his hands to reveal a fat, disgruntled frog.

It was a profoundly unsettling experience for the boys, and it marked the beginning of a long period of questioning their beliefs. They later became Christians, and in 1987 Charles received a letter from an American Christian worker who had met one of the 'boys' in Belgium. 'He was witnessing for Christ,' wrote his friend, 'and often spoke about you. It is truly amazing what the Lord has allowed you to do for His glory . . . . God bless you real good!'

That lay in the future, however, and Charles and Bryce's work had scarcely begun.

The European Christian community in Morocco was a friendly one, and there were interesting visitors to be entertained – including Lord Maclay, who had been Minister of Shipping in World War I and had financed Bryce's training; Sir Edward Spicer, Director of the Evangelical Alliance; the Bishop of North Africa (who persuaded them to give work and hospitality to several needy people); members of the Fraser-Smith family; and a number of Southern Morocco missionaries, some of whom came to work with Mr Nairn in the dispensary or to hold special Bible classes or meetings in Marrakech.

There were four missionaries working with the Echoes of Service missionary magazine, a Brethren concern serving hundreds of missionaries working all over the world. Those in Morocco were Albert Fallaize, Charles Gabriel, Tom Frears and Harry Ratcliffe, with their wives.

One friendship in particular resulted in an unexpected expansion of the farm's ministry. Visiting Casablanca one day, Charles met Captain Eric Fisk, who was living there with his wife of two months.

Fisk was thirty-three years old, a Christian from his late teens. He had fought in the First World War, but was wounded several times in action and spent a good deal of time in hospitals. After the war, the government had given him a year's training in agriculture, and by 1921 he had his own farm near Carlisle. The large farmhouse kitchen was soon in use for Sunday worship, to which farm workers and neighbours were invited; in due course a Brethren church was established there. Later the situation came to the notice of John Laing, head of the well-known building firm, who donated and erected a place of worship in the nearby village.

At the beginning of 1926 Fisk, who might have felt he had found God's plan for his life, chanced to attend a North Africa Mission meeting. There he became aware that God was calling him to take a quite different path: to work among Moslems in Morocco, as an independent missionary.

Fisk appears to have acted almost immediately. He sold his farm in England, arrived in Casablanca before the end of the year, and began learning Arabic.

In Morocco he met the woman who was soon to become his wife. Dorothy Smith came from the same area of Carlisle, and was working as a nurse with the North Africa Mission. They married in 1928, and two months later, in Casablanca, they met Charles.

At the time, they were contemplating their next move. Dorothy shared Eric's vision for independent missionary work, and they were wondering where they should make their base.

'Have you thought of working in the rural areas?' asked Charles.

Eric shook his head. 'We want to go where the majority of the people are,' he explained.

'On the other hand,' countered Charles, 'all the towns have missionaries already.' He looked at the thronged streets of Casablanca, and then allowed his gaze to rest on the distant plains and hills beyond the city. 'There has been no real missionary initiative yet in the country regions. You'd be a pioneer. I know the need, I see it every day on my farm.'

Eric nodded thoughtfully.

'And,' Charles added, 'I have somewhere in mind that would suit you very well.'

An Arab caravan route carrying travellers from a wide area, including the Sahara and Timbuctoo, passed a corner of the Tabahounite Farm. A *caravanserai* was situated there; an Eastern quadrangular inn, with a great inner court where camel caravans and travellers slept for a night. Charles had realised what an excellent vantage point it would make for the Fisks to establish an evangelistic work and a medical clinic.

The Fisks decided to take up Charles's suggestion. Two acres of land were made available to them, and they built a house and began their work. Those two acres were to see an enduring Christian witness in the prewar years: the house became a compound, and a Moroccan Brethren church began there which eventually grew into a membership of over forty – a unique achievement in the 2,000 mile stretch of North Africa.

Among those who visited the Fisks was the Brethren missionary Albert Fallaize, who was to be one of the great spiritual influences on Charles's life. Fallaize, he recalled in later life, was 'one of the most-loved men in Morocco – and possibly in England, too: he had the Master's

radiance more than any other man I have ever met. There
was not one in a million, or fifty million, like him.'

Charles and Bryce gradually began to make links of
friendship with strategic people in Marrakech and the
surrounding region. The three sons of the Mehnebbi
family spent a day on the farm, and Bryce and Charles in
their turn were invited to spend a day visiting the three
Mehnebbi palaces in and around Marrakech. The head of
the family had been knighted by Queen Victoria for
services to Britain.

Of more technical interest to the two young missionaries, however, was the fact that the Mehnebbis grew the
best melons in the world. The growing areas were kept
under strict surveillance; it was impossible to get past the
guards. Charles and Bryce watched fascinated as their
hosts invited them to sample the legendary Mehnebbi
produce. Before any slice was given to the guests, a slave
carefully removed and destroyed every seed; no possibility must be allowed that others should steal the secret.

Charles gradually got to know and like the Moroccans. He
responded to their spontaneity and natural charity. Both
the Berber and Arab people of Morocco warm the
stranger's heart by the generosity of their hospitality. The
poorest Moroccan will kill his last chicken to feed you.

In manner they are somewhat formal and dignified,
placing great emphasis on courtesy and respect for the
aged. But they have their share of human failings too,
being given to passing the buck, and procrastination. The
Moroccan, Charles discovered, has a gift for making
statements capable of a thousand different interpreta-
tions, and knows a hundred ways of doing nothing. On
the whole they strive for a tranquil and quiet, if
uneventful, life, which probably contributes to the
gracefulness of their movements.

Charles developed his knowledge of the Moroccan
people as he wandered round the Djemma. The world of

the Eastern bazaar is built on the skills of bargaining, and he set himself to learn the art. He was soon an expert.

One day he went to buy a carpet. Selecting a suitable market stall, he told the stallholder his requirements.

The first carpet offered was of poor quality and grossly overpriced. 'That is not good enough even for my dog to lie on,' declared Charles. The stallholder nodded in approval. Here was an opponent on whom it was worth sharpening his skills. He produced another carpet.

Charles examined it, fingered its quality, and checked its workmanship carefully. It was a good carpet, he decided, and would do for his purposes. He began the serious business of bargaining. Keeping his expression composed and a little off-hand, he gestured dismissively at the carpet.

'How much is this?'

'Oh Sir, for this finest of carpets, this wondrous craftsmanship – I am robbing myself. A mere hundred and ten *douros*. For this magnificent carpet!'

Charles snorted contemptuously. 'One hundred and ten *douros*? For *this*?'

The stallholder raised his arms in despair. 'For such a beautiful, long-wearing carpet, I would usually ask one hundred and ten *douros*, it is true, but today, for the English milord, a special price – ninety *douros* only.'

Charles shook his head. 'Impossible!' He began to walk away.

As he had hoped (and expected), the stallholder's voice followed him plaintively: 'Come back, come back!' Charles halted in mid-stride. 'Honour me by drinking tea with me,' said the stallholder. 'We will talk more of this.'

In the clutter behind the stall, tea was poured from a metal teapot – 'Made in England, in your own country' – and poured into quaint glasses – 'These too were made in your country.' It was an age-old ritual, to have refused which would have been regarded as a great insult; it seemed almost a minor matter when the deal was finally struck at fifty-five *douros*, and the two parted with mutual promises of life-long friendship.

CHAPTER THREE
In Royal Service – Les Abda

In 1928, Bryce Nairn married, and it became clear that the Tabahounite farm was too small to support everybody. Charles, being single, volunteered to move on, and at the age of twenty-four took up a new and exciting challenge: he was to be entrusted with the management of thousands of acres of some of the richest soil in the world.

There was a gap of several months between Bryce Nairn's marriage and the time when Charles was to take up his new duties. Charles decided that Bryce and his wife needed privacy at the beginning of their married life, and tactfully moved out to stay with the Fisks.

The months he spent with them were very important ones in his life. They had not long built their home, and indeed had not long been married. But they welcomed Charles, and he was able to observe and participate in the beginning of their ministry.

Fisk was, in Charles's eyes, a man of godly greatness. He admired the fact that the older man, who was of an age when he knew very well the magnitude of the task facing him, had left behind not only a thriving farm but also a thriving church in order to follow God's call. He was a disciplinarian, but a man of simple tastes and warm affection. He tackled his work of preaching the gospel with a driving enthusiasm, and Charles recognised that the source of Fisk's energy was the time he spent reading the Bible and the fact that prayer was constantly on his lips.

His wife, who was setting up her medical work at that time, was an ideal companion whose gifts complemented his.

Fisk taught Charles a great deal about personal evangelism, and shared with him many of his own discoveries. As his status in Moroccan missionary work rose in the years to follow, he freely admitted that the great work being done was not his but God's. Charles never forgot the advice he gave him, at the outset of his own missionary career. 'You are not working for God. God is working. And you happen to be involved in his almighty and divine purposes.'

The time with the Fisks came to an end, and Charles moved to his new job. The estate he was to manage belonged to the Moroccan royal family; it was an extensive valley between two hills, watered by the coastal rains. The Sultan's fertile land yielded two crops each year.

It was jealously protected; neither the French government nor any European had been permitted to buy an acre of land anywhere near it. Charles grew over fifty different crops, including wheat and oats, maize, beans and peas of many kinds, linseed, caraway seeds for flavouring bread, and every type of fruit and vegetable imaginable.

A foreman was overseer of the labour force, which numbered several hundred. A second foreman looked after the animals, a third was overseer of crops and a fourth, overseer of vegetables and fruit. They were all answerable to the manager, or *Muckuddan*; he was answerable to Charles, and Charles was answerable to the Sultan. The Muckuddan was a giant of a man, at least six foot three inches tall, and with an air of studied suave courtesy. But Charles was constantly aware of a mistrustful hatred directed at him from the Moor's dark eyes, and felt certain that his own role as the new supervisor was bitterly resented.

Charles's suspicions were dramatically confirmed when, shortly after arriving, he informed the Muckuddan that he would require two horses. 'I shall need to cover a lot of ground each day,' he explained, 'and I don't want to over-ride a horse and have it drop dead under me.'

The Muckuddan nodded gravely. 'I will find you excellent horses,' he promised, and selected two from the stables. One of them was a large black Arab horse, with an aristocratic head and proud manner. Charles decided that it was either a beauty or a beast, and wondered which. He also wondered why the Muckuddan had not sent for the horse foreman, a quiet, unassuming Arab.

Mounting the animal in the stud paddock, he tried to trot forward. But the horse refused to move. Charles gingerly applied pressure with his sharp spurs. The horse remained motionless. The Muckuddan watched impass-ively. A thin sheen of sweat gleamed on the animal's flank, and it was breathing heavily through slightly flared nostrils.

Determinedly not looking at the Muckuddan, but feeling rather foolish, Charles lowered the reins as he thought furiously what to do next. But as the leather touched the horse's neck, it sprang into a gallop. Clutching the reins and grimly trying to gain his balance, he had no hope of bringing the horse to a halt. With a dread certainty, he realised what had happened. *A powder-play horse*, he thought. *He's given me a powder-play horse.*

The powder-play had been one of the first spectacles that Charles had witnessed at the royal court of Morocco. Magnificent Arab stallions charged across the stud paddock in a ferocious battle-line, their richly-clad riders waving sparkling muskets. At the end of the paddock he and the other guests sat with the Sultan. Nearer and nearer came the thundering hooves, until at the last breathtaking moment the riders released a volley of musket shots and reared the horses up on their hind legs only yards away from the stage.

Charles knew what he was in for. The Muckuddan had engineered a well-nigh perfect 'accidental' murder. He imagined the scene later: 'It was an accident, Excellency; he must have borrowed a horse – if only he had asked me! I would have warned him not to take that one . . .'

He had no control over the beast, and it could be only a matter of seconds before the horse reached the climax of its well-rehearsed performance. He had no doubt that the horse would rear, if only to avoid crashing into the deserted stage. He would be at the very least severely wounded by the thrashing hooves, and could easily be killed if he did not fall cleanly from the horse.

There was only one chance, and Charles took it. Dropping the reigns, he grasped the thick mane and held on tightly with his knees. Somehow – he never understood how he had done it – he managed to remain on the horse, and avoided being flung over its head or thrown to the ground.

It was not long before the tables were turned on the Muckuddan, and he received the retribution that was due to him.

The crops were very heavy that harvest-time, and Charles hired a threshing machine. Its owner, a Dutchman, came to stay with Charles in his quarters in one of the royal palaces. It was a superb arrangement; instead of Moorish food, the Dutch couple brought with them tinned asparagus and other vegetables and excellent tinned fruit of every variety, all from Holland. Charles felt, as he was not to feel very often afterwards, that he was living in a style appropriate to a royal palace!

He was watching the threshing one day from a distance, out of sight of the Muckuddan. He observed the manager berating a labourer for idleness; the man was struggling to lift the heavy sheaves into the machine, and was not making the progress the Muckuddan demanded. The man tried to go faster, but the manager was not satisfied. Turning, he seized a pitchfork and thrust it viciously into the labourer's buttocks.

Charles did nothing then, but returned to his quarters in the palace and wrote a letter. He sealed it ceremoniously and dispatched it that night to the Sultan by special messenger. Within twenty-four hours, the Muckuddan came to Charles and asked, with great politeness, if he could be excused for the day, as he had to go and see the Sultan. Charles never saw him again, and if he wondered what punishment had befallen him, he reckoned it was no less than the scoundrel deserved.

The people of Les Abda were mostly of pure Arabian blood, of great dignity and character. Their lineage went back to Ishmael, the son of Abraham and the ancestor of whole Arab nation. Charles became very friendly with them, to the extent that they permitted him to observe a religious ceremony conducted in the middle of the night, in the privacy of individual families.

He was astonished to find that the ritual might have been taken straight from the Old Testament. A lamb was slaughtered, and the blood was wiped on the lintel and door posts of each one-room house or hut. The whole lamb was then roasted in an earthen oven. Afterwards there were entertainments through the night. Charles watched fascinated as two young men, seated on a camel facing each other, engaged in a pillow-fight. It was a long way to the ground for the loser.

He asked the Arabs why they performed the sacrifice. 'For protection,' they explained.

'Where did the custom come from?'

'We have no idea,' they said. 'It has always been done this way with us.'

Charles reached for his Bible and read to them from Exodus 12:7–9. They were amazed. It was one of many opportunities that Charles had to share his Christian faith with his Moroccan friends. And it had arisen from a personal relationship, built on working together on the Sultan's farms. The concept of 'tent-making' missionaries was proving effective.

The next morning, Charles was preparing to go back to his quarters when a colossal heat wave hit the village area. 'I must get back to the palace,' he said.

'That would not be wise,' they assured him.

'I must make sure that the labourers have instructions and that the machine is running properly. I will make haste, I will be back at the palace before the heat strikes.'

A young man appeared, carrying a rolled-up carpet. 'No,' he insisted, 'you would not be able to travel. Come, I will take you to a good place.'

Protesting, Charles gave in. Before they left, the young man gave his wife detailed instructions. 'Chop two onions, and boil them for two minutes. Then bring them to us at *Sidi Barrani's* place.'

They came to a very solid structure. As the young man opened the door Charles saw walls at least a metre thick. Inside, it was spotlessly clean, and cool and dark. The man unrolled the carpet on the floor. 'You will have to stay here until the heat wave has passed,' he said firmly.

His wife appeared at the door holding a steaming cup. 'Drink,' the man said. It was more of an order than an invitation. Charles meekly obeyed.

'Nobody will be harvesting until nine o'clock tonight, when the moon has risen,' the man said. 'I will call for you at eight.'

Left alone, Charles drank the remainder of the onion broth and stretched out on the carpet. Being up the previous night was beginning to take its toll. Waves of heat seemed to seep in through the massive walls, and very little sound penetrated the solid door. 'Lot of fuss,' grumbled Charles, and knew no more until he woke to find the young man shaking his shoulder and the temperature much cooler.

'Thank you,' said Charles. 'I appreciate your kindness. But I would have managed.'

The young man shook his head. 'Several people died today,' he said. 'You would never have succeeded in reaching the palace. No European could have done it.'

Charles digested the information thoughtfully. 'Tell me – what was the building where I slept?'

'It was the tomb of one of our saints. You slept in the cupola.'

He was accepted by most of his Moroccan colleagues, but in one respect he was regarded as odd. He was a successful farmer, employed and trusted by the King, and in his mid-twenties. Yet he was still unmarried. It was not something that worried him, but occasionally he caught his Moroccan colleagues, surrounded by their large families, looking at him with a mixture of pity and concern.

He found his thoughts wandering back to Paris, to a girl who had been a member of the same tennis club as himself. She was from Yorkshire, and he remembered her attractive singing voice. One Sunday she had come to the Institute Biblique, conducted the service and given an excellent talk. At the time he had had no romantic thoughts about her at all, and as he remembered her in Morocco he recalled her extremely slender figure – his Moroccan friends favoured plump wives.

Yet he found himself thinking about her more and more. He knew she had joined the North Africa Mission, and was now working in the Mission House Dispensary at Casablanca. Her name was Blanche Ellis.

At first he thought of her as a helper in his work. He knew that her home was in Leeds, and that she had had three years business training in the shipping industry. She would certainly be able to help him in his business correspondence, he reflected, and her missionary training meant that she would be in full agreement with his industrial missionary aspirations.

He could not get her out of his mind. One day he spruced himself up, saddled his horse, and went to Casablanca to call on Blanche. He invited her out to lunch, and afterwards they walked down a golden beach at Anfa, a few miles outside the town, where a European hotel had just been built which was, after the outbreak of war, to be the location for the Casablanca meetings between Churchill and Roosevelt.

But it was under a peaceful sunset that Blanche and Charles talked that evening, sitting on a rock looking out to the dark Atlantic. They talked long and seriously. By the end of the evening they knew that God had brought them together. A fortnight later the couple were engaged to be married, the wedding date set for six months ahead. It was the beginning of a great working partnership, founded, Charles recalls, 'on faith in Christ, and human love . . . She was a wonderful woman.'

CHAPTER FOUR
Marriage and Khemisset

At Les Abda, Charles knew that he would have to move out of his bachelor quarters at the palace as soon as possible and find somewhere suitable for a married couple.

The harvest was over, and the farm year was coming to one of its natural slack points, so Charles decided it was a good time to resign. He left the Sultan's service with regret, knowing that he was leaving good friends and partners.

He needed advice as to his next step. He had some money of his own saved, and the obvious thing to do was to set up his own farm. But where, and how, with limited financial resources? Then he thought of a Christian friend living in the coastal town of Rabat, Leslie Robinson, a worker with the North Africa Mission. He had a sound business mind, which was not surprising; his father was the director of a well-known food firm in Britain, and his wife was the daughter of a wealthy children's clothing manufacturer.

Leslie was intrigued by Charles's vision of farming as a natural means of making contact in missionary work. He also informed Charles that he was willing to invest capital in such a project, and the two of them went off to look for a suitable property.

Charles felt he would like to establish his farm among a large Berber tribe in Central Morocco, only fifty kilometres east of Rabat. The Berbers were the original inhabitants of Morocco. The French governing centre for the Zemmour tribe was at Khemisset. On the day that Charles and Leslie began looking for land, they found a man in a village four kilometres south of Khemisset who wanted to sell four hectares – about ten acres.

Buying the land was simple, a matter of going with the man to the French Land Bureau office in Khemisset, signing the necessary papers, and handing over the money. While in the office, they learned of a French government scheme whereby plots of land were to be given free to foreigners in Khemisset, the only stipulation being that a house of a certain value must be erected on the land. The scheme was designed to create a European community alongside the houses and gardens of the French governing officials.

Charles chose a plot next to a property belonging to the Gospel Missionary Union of America. A Mr and Mrs Swanson were living in the house, and they offered Charles accommodation while he built his own home. Mr Swanson and a colleague, Mr Enyart, had spent the past two years travelling around the region in native clothes, living as the Moroccans did and preaching the gospel to them. They both married at about the same time. Enyart and his wife went to nearby Meknes, and Swanson settled in Khemisset with his wife, where he was now working ten hours each day translating the entire New Testament into colloquial Arabic. It was work of superb quality, especially the intricate calligraphy.

Charles and Leslie returned to Rabat well satisfied with the day's results, though they knew that it would take at least two years to buy enough parcels of land, around the four hectares already purchased, to make a viable farm.

The next morning Charles moved in with the Swansons, and that afternoon drew up rough plans for a house and took them to the French Government Architect in Khemisset. The Architect made some alterations and improvements, passed the plans as acceptable, and recommended a native builder who had recently arrived from Algeria. Within twelve hours, the builder was at work with a gang of men.

The house was ready two weeks before the wedding, which took place in England. There was no time to travel back by boat, so Charles took a bus to Tangier, sailed to Algeciras, and travelled by train through Spain and France and so to England and Leeds.

Charles and Blanche spent a tranquil five days honeymoon walking on the Yorkshire moors, and within seven days from the wedding, they were back in Khemisset. Blanche began to turn the new house into a home, and Charles purchased additional units of land, at the same time brushing up his Arabic and studying the Qur'an and the Islamic faith.

By the end of eighteen months, Charles had acquired a total of about 100 hectares (about 250 acres) from thirty different Berbers, and it was all in one piece, though the boundary was a peculiar shape. The farm was registered with the French government as 'Sunset Farm', and was positioned south of Khemisset and north of the Middle Atlas mountains.

Six months later, Charles had planned and built a house on the farm with Moroccan labour. Stone and sand were plentiful on the property, and all that needed to be bought was lime and cement for the mortar. He used a method he had devised on the Tabahounite farm; moulds, for shaping earth-and-straw bricks which dried in the sun. The whole process was the same as that used 3,000 years earlier, when the people of Israel made bricks for Pharaoh. Now on his own farm he produced similar moulds, and used them to make concrete blocks. For the house walls themselves, however, remembering his experience during the freak heat wave in Les Abda, he used stone, and made the walls eighteen inches thick against the heat.

The whole building was covered with a strong, flat, reinforced concrete roof. Completing it, Charles realised that if he continued the wall up for another four feet, and added a temporary corrugated iron roof until he could afford a more attractive tiled one, he would have an excellent storage area for his grain crop which no thief could break into or rats or mice succeed in penetrating. Under the house, he also arranged a cellar, which was extremely useful in the hot weather.

Water was a necessity, and a well was sunk near the house which turned out to be capable of supplying all they needed. The construction tested Charles's ingenuity; the subsoil was very sandy, and a system of concrete shell sections had to be invented to stop the walls from collapsing in.

The management of Sunset Farm was also innovative. Charles had spent all the money he had, as well as that invested by Leslie Robinson, in the purchase of land and in building. To finance the running of the farm, he took on thirty Berbers on a co-operative basis. Each already had a few hectares, animals and a plough; they were eager to find more land to produce grain. So Charles divided his land into plots of about three hectares each – an easy matter, as there were no hedges at all, and the plots were marked out in the traditional way by driving in corner stakes.

It was a good system: the more workers, the faster sowing and harvesting would be, and Charles would be freed to tackle other tasks. And it meant that he and Blanche would have all the contact they could wish for with local tribespeople and their families.

The conditions of the partnership were simple. The Berbers supplied the animals and implements for ploughing and sowing, and all the labour. After harvest, each evening at the threshing floors, the grain was divided: one-third was taken as Charles's share, and two-thirds was divided between the Berbers. Charles's only capital outlay was the cost of the land, and the Berbers were able to expand their own farming without the need to find money to purchase land. The contract was drawn up on parchment, and as none of the Berbers could write his name, each man placed a thumb print on the document and an Arab scribe, who was there to read the contract to them, wrote their names alongside the marks.

Partnership was a crucial element in all Charles's projects, partly because he was not a wealthy man, and partly because working closely with the Moroccans was a key reason for him being in the country at all. In the Tabahounite enterprise, Charles and Bryce had had seven partners, but the partners provided only labour, and so received only a fifth of the profits. Their labour was needed for the constant irrigation. In Les Abda, the Sultan provided everything, and his partners received a tenth of the profits.

This method of working with national partners gave the Moroccans the interest and incentive to work hard, and provided natural contacts for Charles and Blanche as 'industrial missionaries'. It avoided the pattern of missionary work sometimes seen, of 'the gospel in one hand and a stick in the other'.

Contacts with local officials also increased. In Khemisset, the Head of Water and Sewage Works, a conscientious and likeable Frenchman, was a keen gardener who grew impressive fruit. He came to the Fraser-Smiths for Christmas dinner several times, and had a special love for Christmas puddings – usually accepting three helpings. It was an opportunity for Charles and Blanche to share their faith at a time of social pleasure and happiness.

Another Frenchman taught Charles a valuable lesson. He was the Chief Judge of the area. Charles was selling green tea to Berber merchants on credit. His first purchaser did not pay by the requested time, and it was soon obvious that he was well practised in delaying tactics. When he realised what was going on, Charles foresaw all his customers following suit. So he went to see the Judge to ask his advice.

'What is the man's name?' asked the Judge.

Charles told him.

'Come back here in a week's time.'

A week later, Charles arrived and was instructed to sit next to the Judge. The customer was called in from an anteroom and began to give a plausible account of himself. His excuses were cut short.

'Take him to prison.'

The next prisoner was called in, and Charles, thinking the matter was over and his money lost, rose to go. The Judge motioned him to remain seated. Charles sat down again, depressed; he had not come to Morocco to accumulate enemies. The second case was dealt with.

'Next!'

Charles looked to see who the third prisoner was. It was his customer, smiling ruefully, holding the payment in his hand. Afterwards, he bore no grudge. In fact, recognising and admiring firmness (as Berbers do), he became a life-long friend.

Charles was profoundly interested in the Berber people, whose laws and customs went back centuries before the birth of Christ. They are a race originating in Palestine, and spread through Asia Minor and Southern Europe, eventually settling in Morocco. They have a proud history, and were never conquered by the Arabs. However, for reasons that are not known, they accepted Muhammed as religious leader, though they never submitted to the laws of the Qur'an, retaining the Abrahamic laws of 1800 BC.

Charles witnessed, for example, the slaughter of a lamb as a peace-offering between enemies;[3] and when Blanche gave birth to a son, Brian, a feast was held with the thirty Berber partners. When the feasting was over, Charles invited them to choose an Arabic name for the child.

'You are not the usual European "Christian", believing in nothing,' they said. 'You truly believe in God. Therefore the child should be called *Abd Allah* – the slave of God.' In the conversation that followed, Charles was able to explain the difference between following Muhammed and following Christ.

There were many such opportunities to live out the Christian life in front of his Moroccan partners, and to observe the many parallels between the Moroccan world and that of biblical Palestine. An example was the occasion when a shepherd, taking his large flock of sheep to the Middle Atlas Mountains for summer grazing, asked permission to camp with them for the night on the Khemisset farm. Charles readily agreed, and that evening, after the visitor had lit his campfire, eaten his meal and brewed green tea, Charles went and sat with him for a while.

'How will you know none of the sheep are missing when you leave tomorrow? Will you count them?'

'I don't need to,' he replied. 'I just look at them. I know if any face is missing.'

Charles was immediately reminded of the words of Jesus Christ, called the Good Shepherd, who said, 'I know my sheep and my sheep know me' (John 10:14). He remembered how those words continued: 'There shall be one flock and one shepherd' (v.16). That was the message he had come with to Morocco: the message of the Shepherd who had promised, 'I lay down my life for the sheep' (v.15).

Bible verses often came to mind, too, in the daily life of the farm; the descriptions of the kingdom of God ('It is like a mustard seed . . .', Mark 4:31), and above all the descriptions of harvesting:

A man scatters seed on the ground. Night and day, whether he sleeps or gets up, the seed sprouts and grows, though he does not know how. All by itself the soil produces grain – first the stalk, then the head, then the full kernel in the head. As soon as the grain is ripe,

he puts the sickle to it, because the harvest has come
(Mark 4:26–29).

In Morocco, the age-old method of sowing by hand was
still practised, and threshing and gleaning were carried out
just as they were in the days of Ruth, over three thousand
years ago. Approaching the harvesters with the traditional
greetings of *Salaam al' ekoom* ('Peace be upon you') and
Allah ekoom maakoom ('The Lord be with you'), Charles
was greeted by the same response from his partners that
the harvesters made to Boaz as he arrived at the fields
where Ruth was working: *Allah yeebarak feek* ('The Lord
bless you!').

The biblical parallels were numerous. Charles's harvesters, cutting by sickle as in Old Testament times, carried
the sheaves on their backs, in a light willow frame, to the
threshing floor. Just as Boaz slept at his threshing floor to
guard against theft, so did Charles. Just as Ruth gleaned
in Boaz's fields, so did the women glean anything that was
dropped by the harvesters.

When all was gathered in, threshing techniques dating
back to biblical times were used. Each morning at sunrise
sheaves would be laid two feet deep on the threshing floor
to bake in the sun. At about mid-day, a team of animals
would be harnessed in line abreast and driven round and
round, their hooves treading the corn from the ears.

When the apostle Paul wrote to the Christians in
Corinth, he used the same process to illustrate his
teaching: 'It is written in the Law of Moses: "Do not
muzzle an ox while it is treading out the grain."' (1 Cor.
9:9). In other words, the beast of burden must be allowed
to eat while it is working, so that it will not collapse from
hunger.

Winnowing was done at about two o'clock most
afternoons, when the light breezes sprang up. The grain
and broken straw were tossed together into the air, the
breeze took the chaff away, and the clean grain fell in a
heap on its own. When there was no wind at all, Charles's

workers used large fans, a practice which might lie behind
Isaiah's reference: 'The oxen . . . and the young asses . . .
shall eat clean provender . . . winnowed with the shovel
and with the fan' (Isa. 30:24).

In his later writings, Charles often drew upon his
Moroccan experiences to illuminate biblical texts; for
example Matthew 3:12 – 'His winnowing fork is in his
hand, and he will clear up his threshing floor, gathering
the wheat into his barn and burning up the chaff with
unquenchable fire.'

And he often drew parallels between his harvests in
Morocco, and the New Testament warnings of the time
when believers and unbelievers would be separated on
God's threshing floor.

The years spent at Sunset Farm were happy ones. Charles
and Blanche were finding increasing opportunities to
teach the gospel and witness for Christ among the
Berbers, Arabs and the European population; and they
had the delight of watching their small son as he grew into
a lively, inquisitive toddler (though the tribesmen had
given him an Arabic name, Charles and Blanche had
decided he ought to have a European name for general
use, and had called him Brian).

They had very little contact with other missionary
societies. Charles received a visit from a representative of
one society asking whether he would consider joining
them, or at least becoming a consultant. But the work of
building up the farm was very demanding, and caring for
the workforce left no room for outside commitments.
Blanche, too, was busy; in addition to caring for Brian,
she did some medical work and organised sewing classes
and Bible readings for women.

But they did not lack visitors at Sunset Farm. Dr
Fothergill, who led tours in Morocco, sometimes arrived
for a Berber meal in a nomadic flat tent – made of goats'
hair and impervious to rain, such tents would have been
perfectly familiar to Abraham. Parties from Scripture
Union visited from time to time.

For their holidays, the family went either to Tangier, or were the guests of Albert Fallaize, who lived at Sale, adjoining Rabat. His house was near the coast, with welcome sea breezes and golden beaches, and Fallaize always made his house available to missionaries when he himself was away. The Fraser-Smiths kept up their friendship with him and also with the Fisks, whose work at the Tabahounite Farm had by now necessitated enlarging the original property into a compound.

In 1935, they had an interesting and stimulating holiday. The Republicans were ruling Spain, and the country was enjoying religious liberty. The Fraser-Smiths went to the first Protestant Congress ever to be held there, and met Sir Kenneth Grubb, a Christian and a leading authority on Latin-American and Spanish affairs. Sir Kenneth's interpretation of current political developments in Spain was disturbing.

Time passed. There were shadows descending upon Europe. Deeply troubling reports of developments in Spain, Germany, Italy and other countries appeared in the newspapers and on radio news broadcasts.

The Fraser-Smiths continued their work in Central Morocco.

The Shortridge family, who had come to live in Khemisset in the Swanson's house after the Swansons left, became close friends. The Shortridges had two little girls, and had adopted an orphaned Moroccan boy, who often stayed with the Fraser-Smiths and enjoyed playing with Brian. Once a month the two families held an English service together at the farm. Every Sunday afternoon, Charles's Berber partners would gather at the house to drink green tea and hear Charles read the Scriptures. They listened attentively, but, so far as Charles could tell, remained unmoved.

Charles did not despair of them, however. It was a door that was always open. Religion was a favourite topic of conversation among the Berbers. Once Charles was in conversation with one of their rulers. The Caid, as the ruler was called, reminisced about attempts to make his Berber tribe a strict Islamic state. The Sultan's *Imam* had been forced to abandon his task, as his activities were causing the threat of a Berber uprising and civil war.

Why then, asked Charles, if the Berbers were so opposed to Islam, had they not embraced the Christian faith?

The Caid smiled his proud aristocratic smile. 'My tribe has never accepted, and will never accept, the laws of the *Qur'an*,' he said. 'And neither have they accepted, nor will they accept, any other belief at all.'

The resolute unbelief of the gentle, courtly Berber leaders was a continuing sadness to Charles. Indeed, in later life he was to reflect that in the decade he spent in that area, he encountered only one believer among the leadership of the tribe, and he had doubts whether that leader was of true Berber descent.

His name was Sheikh Ali, a much-admired raconteur who was fond of singing local ballads, strumming his own accompaniment on a guitar, until in his later years arthritis prevented him from playing. Charles arranged for a hut to be built for him on the farm. Sheikh Ali would stay a week at a time, and Charles visited him, reading the Bible with him and drinking green tea with mint that the Sheikh grew for the purpose; but then he would be gone, a wandering minstrel in the Middle Atlas Mountains, telling Bible stories to the villagers and singing to them about Jesus.

In 1936, the pattern of life at Sunset Farm changed when an SOS was received from a Mr Elson, who ran the Raymond Lull Orphanage Home outside Tangier.

> I am in poor health, and the number of boys in my care has dwindled to ten. I am in desperate need of a long furlough. Would you possibly consider taking over while I am away?

They discussed it and prayed about it, and decided to accept the challenge. They looked after the orphanage for nearly two years, and built it up to thirty-five boys. Once a month, Charles went back to Sunset Farm to see how the Berber manager he had appointed was getting on.

Their assistant in Tangier was a Christian Moroccan with whom they had an excellent relationship. He met and fell in love with a Christian woman working with the North Africa Mission, and they married in the chapel of the house adjoining the Mission.

There were several acres of land around the orphanage; Charles lost no time in organising the boys and teaching them how to reclaim it and grow vegetables. These were sold to the English and French community in and around Tangier. Before long, the orphanage was virtually self-supporting.

The property was perched on a high hill on the coast, seven miles from Tangier. One day in July 1936 Charles was summoned by the boys to look at a large fleet of boats passing out to sea, moving in the direction of Spain. They were laden with Moroccan troops from the Spanish Protectorate in Northern Morocco. Charles and the boys watched the fleet out of sight, and later heard gunfire as the troops disembarked in Spain. Franco had struck; the Spanish Civil War had begun.

The period for which they had agreed to look after the orphanage was coming to an end, when one day the Fisks approached them with a request. The work on their compound had absorbed them for several years. They were physically and spiritually exhausted. They needed to get away for a rest, if they were not to collapse and leave the work unfinished. Would the Fraser-Smiths consider temporarily taking over the leadership of the compound and the growing church of Moroccan Christians?

They had something else to ask as well. Would Charles and Blanche be prepared to start an orphanage on the compound? It was a need of which the Fisks had become very aware, and now the Fraser-Smiths had acquired the necessary experience.

This request called for a major decision: what had been a temporary diversion from farming looked like becoming a change of direction, at least for a few years. Again they prayed and talked the matter over, until they sensed God telling them that this was the next step in his plan for their lives. But as soon as the decision was made Charles realised that it would be unrealistic to be a part-time farmer as well. He arranged to let Sunset Farm to tenants for three years.

When the Fisks returned from their furlough, Charles and Blanche decided they should take a holiday themselves. When they came back, early in 1939, they moved into their old house in Khemisset to wait until Sunset Farm was available again.

In Europe, events were moving towards catastrophe. Franco's Spain was a very different place from that which the Fraser-Smiths had visited in 1935; protestant freedoms had been dramatically curtailed. In Germany, Adolf Hitler's territorial ambitions and crusade against the Jews had both become apparent; and in Italy, Benito Mussolini's regime had begun to impinge on North Africa.

But in Morocco, the Fraser-Smiths were full of plans. Their experiences on the compound and in Tangier had made them decide that they would establish an orphanage themselves, on the farm at Khemisset. They would work in the faith that from such an orphanage would go young Christians and Christian couples who would be a witness for Christ throughout Morocco.

It was a wonderful prospect. It seemed to draw together everything that Charles and Blanche were interested in, good at, and committed to. The first steps were taken to prepare for the establishment of the orphanage. Charles was soon busy with the administrative and practical details, planning the negotiation of Moroccan bureaucracy and casting an experienced eye over the available resources and deciding what extending, rebuilding and refurbishing needed to be done. Blanche, whose family was about to be dramatically extended, began to make her plans too: the children would need to be fed, clothed and taught.

They were required to call on all their previous experience, and what they did not know, they improvised. Long hours, hard work and much prayer brought them to the point where the preparations were complete.

Then, at seven o'clock one busy morning at home in Khemisset, Charles switched on the radio and heard the sombre voice of Turkish Radio announcing the news of Italy's declaration of war.

CHAPTER FIVE
The Voyage Home

As a European with contacts, Charles's opinions of the latest developments were often sought as the war gathered momentum. Paris fell on June 14, 1940; Marshal Pétain was installed on June 16; on June 22, France signed an armistice with Germany. On June 24 the new French Vichy-based Government signed an armistice with Italy. Among the armistice terms was the withdrawal of all French colonies from the war. The radio was full of propaganda, and it was sometimes difficult to decide whether a particular news story was true or false. A particularly bad moment was when the news was announced that the *Ark Royal*, the British Navy's prized aircraft carrier, had been sunk in action.

On the collapse of France, Charles was approached by a group of retired French officers and colonists. Their spokesman, Commandant Hugot, explained their position.

'We have little trust in General Nogues.'

Charles did not register surprise. Nogues, the French Governor-General of Morocco, was a known Fascist sympathiser, and likely to do all in his power to help the German and Italian cause. 'What will you do?' he asked.

'We will stay where we are. We will be a resistance force fighting here in Morocco.'

'I'll ring the British Embassy,' Charles promised.

A frustrating sequence of events followed. The British

Consul-General at Rabat, some miles away on the coast, responded to Charles's telephone call curtly. 'No orders from London as yet – no orders regarding resistance.'

'What d'you think I should do, then?' demanded Charles. 'Should I clear out and get to England and get into the war from there?'

'Sorry – no instructions received. You'll have to wait. Stay put where you are. On no account make a move until things are clearer.'

Charles put the telephone down with a grunt. He was far from happy. Within hours he was in Rabat, chatting to an Arab friend.

'What do you make of all this?' he grumbled. 'Stuck here, can't do a thing, and everybody told to stay where they are. Consul's orders. Wish the Consul would make up his mind.'

The Arab smiled tranquilly, gazing out to the un-troubled, sparkling waters of the Atlantic. 'Oh, I think the Consul has made up his mind.'

'What do you mean?'

'I heard he has just sent his wife and family to America.'

Charles was furious, and immediately decided to abandon official channels. Certainly he did not intend to follow the Consul's advice and sit quietly in Morocco, producing food for export to Vichy France and thence to the German forces. He and Blanche talked late into the night. In all their discussions, the idea of returning to England recurred.

They looked at all aspects of what such a decision would mean, and weighed the advantages against the disadvantages. Eventually they made up their minds. Charles decided to go to Casablanca and arrange a passage to England for himself, Blanche, and Brian. It was a decision that other Europeans were making; Albert Fallaize, Charles Gabriel and their wives also decided to go to England. Charles made the necessary arrangements to put Sunset Farm for the duration of the war into the hands of Ben Kudda, the Moroccan partner who had been left in charge when the Fraser-Smiths had gone to the Tangier orphanage.

The port of Casablanca has become a romantic byword, chiefly due to Hollywood. The famous 1942 film starring Humphrey Bogart and Ingrid Bergman captured something of the atmosphere of the town two years later, when it was crammed with war refugees desperately trying to obtain visas for America. But when Charles arrived in June 1940, there was only the normal bustle and confusion of a Moroccan city.

He was fortunate enough to find quickly a Norwegian boat, the SS *Varenberg*, bound for England with a cargo of phosphates. He arranged a passage immediately with the Captain. The Fallaizes and Gabriels were also booked on the same ship. Charles telephoned Blanche. 'Pack all you can into three suitcases, and come to Casablanca.'

The paperwork for the voyage was complicated. It was necessary to visit the British Consul in Casablanca. Charles found him preoccupied with a telephone call to the French Governor-General. Waiting in an ante-room, he could not avoid overhearing what was said.

'If you will help, Britain will make immediate delivery of aeroplanes and war supplies. We will deliver to Casablanca. Your role would be to lead the resistance against Germany.' The Consul's voice was edgy with frustration, and his tone of authority was tinged with pleading. But it was no use. Nogues had other intentions; he wanted to establish good relations with Vichy and the German-Italian Axis, and was not prepared to provide a base for resistance activities. Eventually the Consul gave up, and remained angrily business-like and aloof when he finally called Charles in to complete necessary formalities.

Nogues's refusal to help Britain cost many lives and no doubt added months to the war. It would have made an enormous difference had British supply ships to Malta and Egypt had air cover in the Mediterranean from the coast of North Africa. In the event, over 80% were lost or damaged, and the long route round the Cape caused lengthy delays for urgently needed supplies. Matters were made worse by the fact that most of the leaders of French colonies and protectorates followed French Morocco's lead and refused to help Britain to resist Germany.

The Fraser-Smith family was soon reunited at Casablanca. Stringent controls were in force. Individuals were permitted to take only 3,000 francs (about £30) out of the country, and outgoing passengers were searched before embarking.

Charles was carrying a small automatic pistol, which he had bought when he began his duties looking after the farmlands of the Moroccan royal family. A gun had been necessary because of the large quantities of cash that he had had to deal with, and he felt it might well come in useful in this new situation.

As the search proceeded and came closer and closer to Charles, he realised that it would probably be confiscated. While the officers were busy with the man next in line he took a large handkerchief from his pocket with the gun wrapped inside it. When his turn came to be searched, Charles was blowing his nose unobtrusively.

The departure from Casablanca, for all its glamour when viewed from the comfortable distance of almost half a century, was a nerve-wracking experience. It was also, as Charles was to remark many times afterwards, a remarkable example of God's providence. Indeed, in that the family got out of Casablanca at all, it was a miracle. Had they been delayed a few weeks or even days, things might easily have been much more difficult.

But besides the big miracle, there were other indications that God's hand was on the Norwegian craft. The only other passengers were Albert Fallaize and his wife and the Gabriels. Albert Fallaize gave great pastoral comfort to passengers and crew during the lengthy and often dangerous voyage. And the Captain, Edward Steen Stenersen, was a remarkable man whom history had thrust into a remarkable role. Most of the Norwegian merchant ships – the fourth largest fleet in the world – were at sea or in foreign ports when Germany attacked Norway in April 1940. This was a windfall for Britain, whose friendship with Norway was strong. 'The Norwegian Government will now use all their resources to help the Allies in their war against Germany,' Churchill told the House of Commons on June 11, and until the entrance of America into the War, Norwegian ships carried 40% of the Allies' petrol requirements. Stenersen was carrying a valuable cargo from a French-controlled port to Britain, and was of considerable interest to the Vichy authorities. Yet he succeeded in leaving Casablanca and managed to bring out a number of refugees as well.

Stenersen, clearly a man of courage and ingenuity, was also an attractive personality: firm and authoritative, but with a sense of humour, and a God-fearing man. Worried that his English passengers might not find the Norwegian staple diet of salted fish palatable, he personally bought a large crate of live chickens and turkeys in Casablanca. They enjoyed fresh meat every day of the voyage.

There were last-minute panics. Just as the boat was about to leave, orders came that the sailing had been cancelled. But fortunately a relief port authority came on duty at that time and Stenersen was able to persuade him to reinstate the order. As soon as the papers were authorised, the crew sprang into activity. Not a moment was wasted. Within minutes, the *Varenberg* had raised her gangplank and pulled away from the quayside. As she headed for open water, the sun began to set.

The waters were busy. A fleet of French naval units had just arrived from France, and the passengers lined the railings of the Norwegian ship, gazing at the huge vessels between which Stenersen was carefully threading his way. They passed the colossal new battleship *Jean Bart*, still under construction. Everywhere there was evidence that Morocco had been chosen by the Axis as a major

maritime base. Charles watched the lights of Casablanca
fade into the shadowy distance, knowing that it was likely
to be a long time before he saw his beloved Morocco and
its people again.

Early the next morning, the boat sailed into Gibraltar
and took on a full load of coal. The voyage to Britain was
usually four days, but in these changed circumstances
Stenersen was expecting it to take from two to three
weeks.

The day that the *Varenberg* spent at Gibraltar provided
thrills both welcome and unwelcome. The sight of the *Ark
Royal* sailing with a fleet of British warships into the port
was exhilarating. It demonstrated that the enemy propaganda machine was dedicated to spreading fear, and the
realisation that the *Ark Royal* had not been sunk was a
great morale-booster. But later that night the family woke
to the sound of menacing aeroplane engines, as the
French Air Force arrived from North Africa on a bombing
mission against the fleet.

It was a retaliatory operation. The British ships had
come from Mers-el-Kebir in Oran, where they had
crippled some of the French warships to prevent them
falling into the hands of the enemy. The French-German
armistice had stipulated that the French fleet was not to
be used by the Germans, but the British were not
prepared to trust that undertaking. Had it been broken,
as other undertakings had been, the German naval
superiority would have been overwhelming.

The *Varenberg* sailed the next day in a convoy with a
cruiser as escort. Stenersen held sealed orders which he
was instructed to open if Spain should come into the war
on the side of Germany while the ship was at sea.

The boat joined a small convoy, led by the cruiser,
which headed out to the mid-Atlantic, well out of reach
of the French coast and the Spanish waters. After
shepherding the convoy well out into the Atlantic, the
cruiser went away to other duties leaving it to take a zig-
zag course to England.

During the long and wearisome voyage, Brian, now eight years old, had the time of his life. He was appointed as crew's mascot, and was usually to be found on the bridge, his small hands grasping the wheel, guided by a friendly crew member who surreptitiously kept a firm hand on the wheel at the same time. Not many of his contemporaries could boast that they had 'steered' a cargo vessel half-way across the Atlantic, and it said much for the gentleness and generosity of captain and crew that a small child, on a dangerous and uncomfortable voyage in wartime, would be able to look back on the experience as one of the most wonderful of his young life.

As the boat approached England, a Sunderland flying boat arrived to escort the convoy home. One boat developed engine trouble and fell behind, and was torpedoed. No rescue operation was possible; it would merely have increased the size of the target for the enemy submarine that had already attacked. While the *Varenberg's* passengers were coming to terms with that news, a German plane appeared and bombed the convoy. The ships escaped with minimal damage. The Sunderland appeared to take no notice, and its guns remained silent.

'Why doesn't it *do* something?' demanded frightened passengers.

'It's got its own job to do,' an officer on board explained. 'These waters are full of U-Boats. The Sunderland's monitoring the sea all the time and it's not a fighter aircraft. Its sole job is to watch out for the subs.'

'What do we do then?'

The sea stood in towers as the bombs exploded frighteningly close to the ships, and the vessels lurched as the waves pitched back and forth in time to the deafening explosions.

'Take what shelter you can,' advised the officer. 'And pray . . .'

Two days away from port, a cruiser came and escorted the convoy to Liverpool. But as they came into harbour there was a last, frustrating delay. A German plane had just dropped floating mines, and the *Varenberg* and its companions had to wait for these to be cleared away before docking and disembarking.

The experience made a lasting impression on Charles, and he frequently praised the Norwegian people for their courage and dedication. Writing in 1984, he acknowledged,

> They were men fortified with a rugged and deeply rooted evangelical faith in God and a righteous cause. They rarely spoke of their religion, and words like 'sacrifice' and 'idealism' were unspoken thoughts. They were men who preferred to express themselves through action. Freedom and love of their country were not things to be talked about. Their actions spoke louder than words. Their endless battling with the fierce Norwegian elements in everyday life made them well-suited to resist an enemy, to value their freedom and doggedly oppose all oppression and deprivation of rights. They were physically equipped for the kind of fighting war required and, being used to the capricious sea and the mountain storms, they faced death as naturally as birth and life.
>
> They were prepared to accept any ordeal. They feared not death, but only the thought that under torture they might give others away.[4]

It was not a judgement based solely on the excellent treatment and care that he and his family received on the hazardous journey from Morocco. Norway was just one nation out of several with which Charles was to come into a close working relationship. The European Resistance fought long and courageously against Hitler's forces, and many of their workers looked to London for support and resources. In this support role, the Government department MI6 played a major part, and it was that department which Charles was about to join.

CHAPTER SIX
Return to England

The Mersey was grey and choppy, the clouds brooding and piling up over the severe buildings of Liverpool's Pier Head as the passengers from the SS *Varenberg* descended the swaying gangplank and stepped onto English soil. A straggle of forlorn, tired people made their way to the disembarkation office, carrying their frugal luggage. All around the docks and landing stages war supplies were piled high ready for despatch to the fronts, and uniformed soldiers and military police were everywhere. It was about five o'clock in the morning, and a chill drizzly mist lay on the river.

Charles and his family were resigned to a long wait as the Naval Reserve conducted the complicated disembarkation procedures. But as they entered the long shed and the queue moved towards the officers at the reception tables, Charles saw the Inspecting Officer and received a jolt of surprise.

'Mr Underwood!'

The Officer beamed. 'Charles! What are you doing here? I thought you were in Morocco!'

Arthur Underwood had been a partner in Charles's uncle's solicitor's practice. It had been several years since Charles had seen him, but he recognised him at once and was delighted to receive such a pleasant welcome on a bleak morning. 'We got out on the *Varenberg*,' he explained, and introduced his wife and son.

The queue behind was long, and there was no time for

a lengthy conversation. 'What are you going to do next, Charles?'

'First I have to change some money.' He reached into his wallet and pulled out the handful of French francs he had obtained at Casablanca. 'I've hardly any English money besides this.'

Underwood pulled a long face. 'You're going to have to move fast,' he said. 'You're only just in time. There's an exchange prohibition coming in at noon. If you haven't changed those francs into sterling by then, you won't be able to – they'll be frozen for the duration.'

There was nothing for it but to take the first available train to London. It was a sombre journey; evidence of war was everywhere, not least in the scarcity of young men. Women were doing jobs that no female had ever done before the war, and some of the men were in uniform or carrying luggage with forces labels.

Making his way through a London already showing the signs of a city at war, Charles arrived at his bank. The cashier looked at the francs dubiously. 'You'll have to take these to the Bank of England, there's a freeze coming up.' The official at the Bank of England shook her head. 'You've been misadvised, Sir. You must negotiate the currency through a bank where you have an account.'

Grumbling furiously, Charles returned to his own bank. 'No, I'm sorry, there's no way I can help you. Our instructions are quite clear. The Bank of England has got things mixed up.'

'This is ridiculous!' Charles exploded. 'We're talking about less than fifty pounds. I shall spend that much travelling between banks if somebody doesn't do something soon.'

'I'm sorry, Sir.' The cashier spread her hands apologetically. 'If I could help you I would. But I can't.'

The noon deadline was looming. In desperation, he forced his way to the Manager's office, fighting his way past awestruck and flustered bank officials who tried in vain to stop him. The Manager listened courteously to the extremely angry young man who had burst into his office, and made arrangements for the currency exchange to take place there and then. Charles left to rejoin his family, still grumbling, clutching thirty pounds. It was all he had to start a new life in England.

'Shall we ring John Laing?'

On the voyage from Casablanca, Charles and Blanche had discussed what their first step should be when they arrived. They had decided that they would contact Laing. He was well-known in Brethren circles, and the Fisks had told Charles about his help when Eric Fisk had farmed in Carlisle and founded a Brethren church there. In 1940 Laing was already a well-known builder and airfield contractor, noted both for his considerable achievements in industry and also for innovative, enlightened management.[5] Among his many unpublicised charitable interests was missionary work in Morocco; he had contributed to the prospective orphanage work at Khemisset.

The warmth of John Laing's welcome dispelled the exhaustion of the long train journey from Liverpool and the tensions and frustrations of the bank problems. 'You must stay at the house in Harrow, of course,' he said. 'It's an unoccupied furnished property that we are able to make available to missionaries on furlough.'

Charles began to explain about his limited finances. Laing interrupted him. 'There is no question of payment. This house is available to you rent-free.'

Charles, Blanche and Brian spent several weeks in John Laing's Harrow house.[6] Charles was anxious about safety, having seen enemy planes in action on the voyage home. In the garden of the house was a corrugated-iron Anderson air raid shelter of the type that had been issued to thousands of families. Charles peered inside it and decided that the wet, cold interior was no place for a family with a small child to shelter in. The same day that they arrived in Harrow, he dismantled the iron sections and reassembled the shelter indoors, in the sitting-room, with a bed beneath it. This offered double protection, from debris and splinters of glass in the event of a bombing near miss, and also from the collapse of the entire house in the event of a direct hit. In addition, the indoor shelter was warm and cosy, and helped to keep the family free from colds and infections as they made the transition from the warmth of Morocco to the British climate.

The shelter was not erected a moment too soon. The following night the London Blitz began in earnest. Charles, having come to England to help the war effort, signed up the next day as a despatch rider, taking messages from one air-raid Civil Defence HQ to another. It was often grim work. One night he was detailed to take a county engineer on the pillion of his motor cycle to inspect an unexploded bomb that was lying in a vital spot. Charles left the engineer assessing the situation and went to telephone the bomb disposal squad. When he returned he found a scene of chaos. The bomb had been a timed device, and it had exploded while he was away. The engineer had been killed outright and his body horribly mutilated.

With the bombs came many casualties – so many that it was not long before a shortage of wood made coffin manufacture extremely difficult. A Harrow man devised a collapsible cardboard version, and it was Charles's job to take it to the appropriate HQ for inspection and approval.

Morale was shaky in some quarters. German propaganda broadcasts were having an effect on parts of the British civilian population. Some people, contemplating the bomb damage and the power of the German Luftwaffe, openly remarked to Charles that they believed it was impossible to win the war. Britain should abandon the struggle, they said, and follow the example of France and Italy and make a separate peace. Charles even heard this defeatist philosophy from a town clerk who was in charge of air-raid defence. He immediately reported the man, who was soon replaced. 'We haven't given up all we had and risked our lives on the Atlantic just to sit and listen to that kind of talk,' he told Blanche.

Laing kept a kindly eye on the family, and gave help in many ways. He even offered Charles a job, and sent a car to bring him to the interview. The war, Laing explained, had brought about an enormous increase in his airfield construction projects. He needed to recruit more staff. Was Charles interested?

Charles was seriously interested in the offer, but after thinking about it decided that airfield construction was not the line of work he should pursue. However, the offer started him thinking about working in industry, and the aircraft business seemed to offer the chance to put his practical skills into action. When a job became available with Avro, he accepted. The Fraser-Smiths left the Harrow home with regret and with much appreciation of John Laing's kindness. He in his turn wrote to them shortly after they had left, complimenting them on the tidy state of the house, and expressing amusement and admiration for the ingenious indoor shelter. 'I could use somebody with a mind like that in my business!' he wrote. It was typical of Laing that he should find time to write something more than a brief note, when the escalating air war was demanding all his time and energies.

The Avro factory was a specially-constructed underground area in Yeadon, on the edge of the Yorkshire moors. Blanche and Brian stayed in Leeds, at Blanche's family home. They were able to pick up old friendships and make new ones, and on Sundays the family was able to attend an Open Brethren evangelical church in Leeds.

It was at this church that Charles one night gave a talk about his work in Morocco, enthralling his audience (which included Professor F.F. Bruce[7]) with stories of his inventive and effective methods and unorthodox pioneering techniques. In the audience was the director of the

Ministry of Supply (MOS) in Leeds, G. Ritchie Rice,[8] and sitting with him was Sir George Oliver, the Director General of MOS in London.

Rice, a committed Christian, was very familiar with missionary work, having served on a number of missionary society committees. He and Oliver spent a few minutes after the lecture chatting to Charles. The next day, when Charles arrived home from Yeadon, there was a message. Would he report to Rice's office that evening?

At the Ministry HQ in Leeds, Ritchie Rice praised Charles warmly. 'Your work in Morocco shows that you've got initiative and inventiveness. And you're flexible, too. You aren't tied to official channels. You find a way to get what you want.'

Charles, unsure what this appreciation was leading to, waited. Rice picked up a pencil. 'I want to know more about your work in Morocco.'

The cross-examination that followed was thorough and detailed. The information Rice demanded was odd – nobody had wanted to know about such aspects of the Moroccan work before. Rice made occasional notes. Eventually he seemed satisfied. 'What exactly are you doing at Yeadon?' he said abruptly.

'Kicking my heels,' replied Charles honestly. 'I'm looking for a chance to get into the War. There's enough to do at Avro, but it's not how I want to spend the duration.'

Rice nodded. 'I've a job coming up that you'd be good at,' he said. 'It needs your kind of brain. One that can cut corners. The civil servants in my department aren't flexible enough for such a job. Are you interested?'

Charles agreed instantly, though Rice was extremely evasive about what the job entailed. All he would say was that Charles would be working for MOS, initially with a colleague whose work involved a specialist knowledge of clothing and textiles. 'You'll be his assistant,' said Rice.

'But the big job will start quite soon. It will be highly secret and highly specialised.'

Within a week, Rice had arranged for Charles to leave Avro and take up work in MOS. Work as a civil servant was if anything less interesting than Avro had been; he spent three weeks handling requisitions and orders for clothing and textiles. Pen-pushing and warehouse control seemed to have only marginal relevance to the war effort, and sometimes Charles wondered if the decision he had made had been a wise one. Perhaps Rice's definition of an exciting job was not the same as his own.

Then he was sent for and required to sign the Official Secrets Act. No explanation was given. He was merely told that his work in Leeds was finished. Ritchie Rice would be moving to London. So would Charles. He was to pack up his family and belongings, and report to MOS HQ in London.

CHAPTER SEVEN
Back to London

Charles, Blanche and Brian settled into Charles's family home at Croxley Green, near Rickmansworth in Hertfordshire. Like many wartime London civil servants, he commuted each day by train. Croxley Green was far enough out of London to be relatively clear of the bombing zones, evacuation of young children was not necessary, and the family was able to stay together during the whole of the war.

Charles was in his late thirties, lean and fit after his years in the Moroccan sun, and itching for something significant to do after the routine work he had been doing in Leeds. As he arrived at Marylebone Station on his first morning and made his way to his new office, he was filled with a keen anticipation.

His instructions were to report at a Ministry of Supply war department; Portland House, London. The building, in Tothill Street not far from the Houses of Parliament, had been requisitioned from the Portland Cement Company. Hidden away next door were the headquarters of the Secret Service, MI6, to whom Charles was to be ultimately responsible. MI9, which was responsible for interrogating enemy prisoners of war, helping British prisoners to escape from behind enemy lines, and helping shot-down airmen to evade capture, was another department with which Charles was to work closely throughout the war.

His office on the first floor of Portland House was

sparse, furnished with little besides a desk and three telephones. His immediate MOS boss, working from an office on the same corridor, was Ritchie Rice. Beyond the knowledge that Charles had some connection with supplying prisoners of war with various requirements, he knew nothing.

Because of his job, Charles avoided becoming too friendly with his colleagues, and remained isolated in his office in the Directors' corridor. As a result he missed at least one extraordinary coincidence: working in the Directorate of Devices of MOS was a man called Walter G. Calvert-Carr. He and Charles had been neighbours in Croxley Green, and as ten-year olds had cycled together to Watford Grammar School before Charles moved on to Brighton College. It was not until decades later that Charles realised that Calvert-Carr had been working a few offices away during the war.[9]

Portland House was a useful front for an operation that needed to keep a low profile. The building had been officially requisitioned by a department known as Clothing and Textiles for the Armed Forces. So far as the other inhabitants of the building knew, Charles was an ordinary temporary civil servant, on the MOS Clothing and Textile payroll. Clothing and Textile's three sections were named CT1 (dealing with clothing for the Navy), CT2 (for the Army), and CT3 (for the Air Force). Charles and those who worked under him were designated 'CT6', as just another section of Clothing and Textiles. The '6' gave a secret clue to the link with MI6 for the few who were in the know.

The true nature of Charles's work has been well described in his *Secret War of Charles Fraser-Smith* and amplified in his other books. It was basically a supply operation, but the goods supplied were highly specialised and the recipients were underground agents, spies, Resistance workers, prisoners of war planning to escape, and others who needed specialised and sometimes previously unheard-of equipment. The original instructions came mainly from MI6; any bulk deliveries from CT6 went direct from the firms to a MI9 depot, from where they were redistributed to MI6, MI9, SOE, SAS and other clandestine groups.

> I was [MI6's and MI9's] floating production and procurement man. My job was to supply material on demand for highly secret and often sensitive projects on behalf of nearly all Britain's Intelligence services. Others did similar work in different fields (Major Clayton Hutton at Beaconsfield, for one), but so far as I know I was the only civilian not assigned to a particular service.[10]

Approximately half the requests for supplies were detailed and precise. Most of the remainder were much more vague, presenting something of a challenge in obtaining the required goods in a situation of wartime shortage and firms working below full capacity and with reduced workforces. About ten per cent of all the requests he received were ones which demanded ingenuity, lateral thinking, and sheer inventiveness. These were the requests which resulted in the 'gadgets' for which Charles was later to become famous.

But fame came long after the war. During the war years, he was simply the junior civil servant who received goods from firms of every description, and who regularly sent harmless-looking parcels out from his office. Even the directors of other departments who shared the same corridor were unaware that he was connected with MI6, or of the extent of his secret activities. Their secretaries, seeing the parcels regularly leaving Portland House, dubbed CT6 the 'Comforts for the Troops' department.

From the beginning, the whole operation was marked by a veil of secrecy and anonymity. Charles, who had never been an office worker, was disinclined towards paperwork, and had no intention of starting now. His records system consisted of a notebook, in which he accumulated a growing list of firms and individuals who could be called on for unusual requirements. All his contact with other departments was by telephone, and his callers introduced themselves by coded names – 'Bro', for example, meant MI6, calling from their offices in Broadway, just around the corner.

The extreme secrecy which surrounded most aspects of Charles's war work is well illustrated by the role of Lieutenant-Colonel Sir Claude Edward Marjoribanks Dansey KCMG, CMG – or, as he was known by Charles and others whose work brought them into contact with him, 'Uncle Claude'. Charles never lost the profound respect for this man that Dansey's wartime activities aroused in him. 'The most important and invaluable man in World War II', Charles was to call him in later life: 'the most powerful man, in many ways, in the country – and he was able to keep his power hidden.'

Dansey's superior, Colonel Stewart Menzies – the political Chief of MI6 – was an ex-Guards officer and a friend of royalty, members of the peerage, and other dignitaries. The appointment of this Old Etonian in 1940 as director of MI6, Britain's major intelligence network abroad, had been greeted with anger and dismay in some quarters. But public discussion of his suitability or unsuitability was out of the question. Such a debate would have been a criminal offence under wartime restrictions, and the Press was forbidden to speculate about such matters.

Indeed, very few people knew very much at all about MI6 or the other secret departments. It was a deliberate and carefully enforced policy. The departments had to remain shadowy and little-known, and the same had to be true of their chiefs. Menzies worked away from the public eye at a desk that was said to have belonged to Nelson, behind a padded door in the unimposing offices in 54 Broadway, opposite St James's Park Underground station.

Yet Dansey, his deputy, was even more secretive. His clandestine operations became a legend in the Secret Service (MI6). In fact, he was the mastermind behind most of British Intelligence work. Menzies was content to be a figure-head, a political rather than a professional appointment. But Dansey was a gifted and single-minded professional. His career in MI6 lasted for forty-five years, for twenty-two of which he was the top brain. His contribution to the war was known to very few.

The advantage of such self-imposed secrecy was that Dansey was able to get on with his work without the enemy knowing that he even existed. It was an advantage that he clung to tenaciously. He never permitted anybody to photograph him. He did not appear in the photographs of his own wedding. When he died, a number of passports, all in different names, were found in his home.

Dansey, whose prewar travels had included trips to Morocco, Spain and Mexico, ran a world-wide network of agents. He masterminded numerous intelligence projects and co-ordinated information flowing in from all parts of the world. He oversaw the setting up of SOE (the Special Operations Executive) in 1940, and made it his business to keep 'eye-control' of the agents working for his own department and those working for the new SOE, which involved travelling. He travelled light and had little use for paperwork. He never interviewed people in his office at MI6 Headquarters, meeting them instead in other Secret Intelligence Service offices, in one of several different flats, or in a 'safe house'.

Charles's work came under the same cloak of anonymity and secrecy. He never sent or received any written order or communication concerning MI6, MI9, SOE, SAS, OSS(CIA) or any other secret section; and it was taken for granted that his staff and Dansey's were to avoid meeting wherever possible, and that in no circumstances were they to enter each others' buildings.

An extraordinary episode during the war shows the superb anonymity of Dansey's operation. Charles never

knowingly met Dansey: his two contacts at MI6 were a
Commander Ridley and a Commander Rhodes. He never
met Rhodes, who remained a voice on the telephone for
the whole of the war. But a meeting with Ridley was
proposed on one rather strange occasion.

Ridley's office was in the Broadway building. One
afternoon, Charles was phoning him on a routine matter.

'I'll get the stuff sent over,' Ridley promised. 'Only
thing is, it'll have to be after five. My chaps are all tied
up. Won't be much later than five.'

'That's not a problem,' replied Charles. 'I'm staying the
night firewatching. I'll be here myself to take delivery.'

Ridley laughed. 'I'm doing a spot of late duty too,' he
remarked. 'Won't be an early night for me either.'

Charles's impish sense of humour asserted itself
dangerously. 'Let's have a bit of light relief later, then.
Why don't we take in a show?'

There was a silence at the other end of the line. Charles
wondered if the joke had been a mistake. He imagined
Ridley's brain working overtime to digest the unheard-of
proposal.

'– Or not, as the case may be,' he added lightly. Light
relief of that kind for fire-watchers in his own department
was an accepted practice. But Ridley worked for MI6.
'No, could be a good scheme. I'll have to check, though.
I'll ring back.' Ridley sounded non-committal.

Later, Ridley's secretary telephoned. 'Commander
Ridley has booked seats for *Madame Butterfly*. He will
wait for you in his car by the tailor's shop at the end of
your street, at seven o'clock.'

The car was waiting as promised, and Charles climbed
in. A taciturn figure in the back seat nodded to the woman
chauffeur, and within minutes they had arrived at the
theatre. Charles took advantage of the short ride to steal
a covert glance at his colleague. Ridley was short, on the
lean side, with sparse balding hair and thick pebble
glasses. Charles estimated his age at approaching sixty,
which slightly perplexed him, as he had expected a

younger man. The few abrupt sentences which Ridley uttered were also difficult to identify with the voice on the telephone. He put it down to the wartime telephone problems.

At the theatre, Ridley hardly spoke beyond remarking that he was very fond of opera; there was no small talk. The two men sat stiffly side-by-side, resolutely watching the performance. Afterwards, they exchanged a few polite words and shook hands. Charles made his way back to the office feeling distinctly odd about the whole experience, and he did not attempt to repeat the experiment with any more of his contacts for the duration of the war. Ridley never mentioned the matter again.

There were more important things to think about, and the incident receded in Charles's mind. Forty years later, the period of official secrecy expired and Charles published the first of his books, *The Secret War of Charles Fraser-Smith*, in 1981. He sent a copy to Ritchie Rice. Rice was astonished to learn of the scale of his wartime activities under Dansey. Officially, Charles was not supposed to have known anybody beyond Commanders Ridley and Rhodes, and Rice had thought he was supplying only MI9.

In the book, he described the visit to *Madame Butterfly*, which clearly still perplexed him.

> I found it strangely awkward to be with him. For some reason it seemed oddly wrong to be with this secret man, as if our relationship was in some way destined to remain at arm's length – a clandestine, cloak-and-dagger affair of clipped telephonic exchanges and coded identities, as though anything more intimate was breaking the rules. Perhaps in the strictest sense it was, certainly he never repeated the process. We did not meet again during the war, or after it, in spite of our joint activities.[11]

While preparing his third book Charles decided to try to

trace some of his wartime telephone contacts and introduce himself to them. Among those he tried to contact was Commander Ridley. He wrote to the Admiralty in the hope that they could provide an address, but received the reply that Ridley had died. However, his son, Admiral Terence Ridley, was living only forty miles away.

Charles telephoned and arranged to call, and an extraordinary conversation followed. The first inkling of doubt came when Terence Ridley expressed great surprise that his father should have suggested going to *Madame Butterfly*.

'He wasn't at all interested in opera,' he explained.

Charles's suspicions were suddenly rekindled. 'Do you have a photograph of your father?'

'There's one upstairs – I'll get it.'

Commander Ridley stared out of the photograph; a tall, commanding figure, well-built and without spectacles. 'He was six foot two,' the Admiral volunteered.

'That solves the opera mystery, at any rate,' declared Charles. 'The man with whom I went to *Madame Butterfly* was not your father. I'd be very interested,' he added thoughtfully, 'to know just who he was . . .'

He found the answer later in a file of newspaper cuttings. There, in a clipping dated 1982, he found a brief paragraph.

This is the first picture ever published of Sir Claude Dansey, the MI6 Chief who, it is now known, was behind the Amiens Prison Raid in February 1944. As a result of this operation more than 700 agents and Resistance men escaped. Among them was the key figure of Raymond Vivant without whose freedom, it seems, D-Day could have had to be postponed for a year.

Looking out from the indistinct newspaper photograph

was the thin, bespectacled figure who had sat next to him at the opera.

No doubt Dansey had taken the opportunity to see for himself the remarkable civil servant from MOS who blithely ignored red tape, produced goods in record time, and thought up ingenious secret devices.

While Charles had been outwitting the Germans, his Chief had been applying strategems incognito. He was curious to have a look at Charles, but under no circumstances could Charles know who he was.

When he realised what had happened, Charles appreciated the deception, and was glad to know that he had, even unknowingly, spent an evening with the man whose work he intensely admired: 'We shall never know what we really owe to him for our victory, as, so far as is known, he kept no records. Indeed, he would not have had time.'

CHAPTER EIGHT
The Second World War

The fascinating story of Charles's work in CT6 is well documented in his books. They record not only his ingenuity, but also the very great contribution made by British and Allied firms that worked outside their normal routines and to highly unusual briefs, so that the work in the battlefield and behind enemy lines could go forward with the best equipment and resources. The books also reveal Charles's intense admiration for the people he served; secret agents, prisoners of war, the Maquis and the Resistance workers. They also celebrate the unnamed individuals who gave them shelter, people who risked home and life itself to give help to those who knocked on their doors in the night.

Charles's career as an author began in his seventies, and his correspondence became substantial as the books circulated widely and readers all over the world wrote with appreciation, questions, or sometimes their own wartime reminiscences. A large proportion of his correspondents were young people, who had discovered Charles either by reading the books or by hearing him speak at a Crusaders meeting, at a church visit or at one of his many visits to schools.

To these young friends and admirers Charles was never 'Mr Fraser-Smith', nor, even for special friends, 'Charles' or 'Uncle Charles'. Universally, he was 'Q', and he joined in enthusiastically, signing his letters 'Q' – often with a Bible verse in Arabic thrown in for good measure, and sometimes, for youngsters or a few friends, changing to 'Q-007'.

The name 'Q' is taken of course from the world of Ian Fleming, whose novels, featuring James Bond (Special Agent 007, licensed to kill), have been made into a number of films which have been enormously popular among the young. In the novels, the man who makes the wonderful gadgets for James Bond is a government boffin named 'Q'.

During the war, the idea that the kind of work he was engaged on would one day become a popular element of large-budget fantasy spy films full of sex and spoof violence would have caused Charles mixed dismay and amusement. The irony of the matter, which did not escape Charles nearly half a century later, is that Charles was Fleming's model for 'Q'.

They met in wartime. Charles was busy with a routine supply project in Portland House when the telephone rang.

'Fleming here – Naval Intelligence. Is that Fraser-Smith of CT6/MOS?'

'Yes. Which section of NI?'

'I'm PA to the DNI.'

The two men slipped easily into the cryptic shorthand of wartime government departments. Fleming was Personal Assistant to the Director of Naval Intelligence. 'I want to come round and see you,' Fleming said.

Charles was intrigued at the prospect of adding another department 'scalp' to his growing crop of contacts with top secret departments. He had already had dealings with MI6, MI9, SOE, OSS(CIA) and SAS. But NI was new to him.

'Yes, certainly,' he said. 'Ten o'clock sharp, room 01, ground floor Portland House.' His own office, tucked away among the Directors of MOS, was out of bounds to all his visitors, and he did not propose to make an exception for the PA to the DNI.

Room 01 could have come itself from the pages of a James Bond novel. Small and sparse, it could only be reached through an outer office, in which two members of staff worked, providing a 'front' and if necessary a bodyguard. He met Fleming there at the time arranged.

'I've been over to Government Communications,' Fleming began. Charles recognised the code-name for MI6. 'I've seen some of your gadgets. They're very good.'

'Thank you,' said Charles, wondering what was coming next.

'Got a job for you, if you can help,' said Fleming. 'Golf balls. You've been using them to hide secret messages, maps, compasses. Very clever. Can you supply me with a few?'

He was a charming man, with many of the elegant characteristics of his famous creation 007, but Charles was unmoved. 'I can't supply you personally,' he said. 'It will have to be done through official channels. You'll have to go through your Director. I can only supply on a note from Admiral Godfrey.'

Charles's brief records do not record whether the requisition ever came from Admiral John Godfrey. But the golf-balls re-appeared many years later in one of the James Bond novels.

He picked up the knife and dug its point into the cover of the ball and levered. A half-inch circular section of the ball came away on the tip of the blade and he passed the ball across the desk to the hunchback, who tipped the contents, three uncut stones of ten to fifteen carats, on to the leather surface of the desk.[12]

It made a good story, but in wartime such golf balls would have lost Naval Intelligence many of its best agents. Charles's creations were crafted by experts, and instead of a hollowed-out cavity had their contents embedded in a properly compounded elastic interior. This had been exhaustively tested by the manufacturers until Charles was satisfied that the ball, with its precious cargo of compass or other equipment, would behave exactly like any other golf ball. You could play golf with an MOS ball. Trying to play with one of Fleming's fictitious creations would have given the game away in an instant.

The character of 'Q' in the novels, a taciturn man with little patience for James Bond's schoolboy jokes and a constant worry that Bond's recklessness would write off the best and most expensive of Q's equipment, was certainly based on Charles. Fleming was very interested in Charles's gadgets, and Charles heard on the departmental grapevine that he had even tried some of them out on his NI colleagues, though how he managed to persuade Ridley and Rhodes of MI6 to allow access to them remained a mystery. However, Charles remembers him as a man of charm and persuasiveness, and has suggested that some aspects of Bond's character – for example, his gourmet appreciation of good food – were drawn from the personality of his creator. Bond's 007 number was taken from Godfrey's departmental filing system: NID/007 referred to top secret documents. An unlikely way for Civil Service pen-pushing to become immortal!

Charles regards the James Bond novels as 'harmless fun', though he intensely dislikes the 'superficial sex encounters'. An interesting aspect of the hugely successful films is that Desmond Llewelyn, who plays 'Q' in them, has an uncanny physical resemblance to Charles, such that photographs of them are often confused. In 1983 Charles visited the TSW studios in Plymouth to make a television programme with Llewelyn, and the two men liked each other at once and were soon swapping anecdotes.

Charles was generous in his praise of Fleming when he mentioned him in his books.[13]

> Fleming was the type we needed. Thankfully, the war brought in all kinds of geniuses.[14]

The last word on the matter can be left with the *Sunday Express*, who in a review of *Secret War* had this to say:

Ian Fleming's James Bond yarns are famous for their ingenious secret weapons and gadgets. But few of his fictional inventions were as cunning as some of the extraordinary gadgets and ploys that were used during the Second World War and dreamed up by Charles-Fraser Smith.

BBC CALLING

The North Africa Campaign was of particular interest to Charles, especially when the TORCH operation with its North African landings was in preparation in 1942.

MI6 and SOE agents were engaged in cloak-and-dagger runs between Gibraltar and the Morocco, Tunisia and Algeria coasts. To aid them, Charles arranged the supply of some of his non-rustling silk maps printed for that area. He also prepared escape kits and other secret equipment for British pilots, officers and special raiding units behind enemy lines.

The imminent North Africa landings reminded Charles of his farming years in Morocco. It seemed to be a lifetime ago, and many things had happened since then of global significance. Yet he recalled the phenomenal success he had had in increasing crop yields with improved irrigation and agricultural techniques. As he thought back, he began to think about the wartime food problems that Britain was now having. Surely there must be a way to make use of the experience he had gained in Morocco to help the North Africans overcome their own food limitations?

Soon he had arrived at an idea. Why not persuade the North African farmers to grow more food? It would bring in money and food for them, and it would reduce the dependence of the Allied Forces on food that had to be imported from further afield, so freeing vital shipping resources for the war effort. He felt sure that the farmers would co-operate, especially if they were given seed and expert help in planning sowing and planting programmes.

He thought the idea through again, looking for snags. There did not seem to be any: the scheme appeared to be water-tight. He reached for the red telephone on his desk. It was his hot-line to the War Cabinet offices.

A few days later he was summoned to face a formidable committee at the Cabinet offices to discuss the proposal.

Charles suggested to the committee that a crop of potatoes and vegetables could, given the right conditions, be raised in a matter of weeks. He proposed that seed potatoes should be sent from Scotland, and seeds for other crops and vegetables should be sent from America, in the bomb racks of war planes.

To his considerable surprise, the committee accepted Charles's proposal without hesitation. Soon cables were being drafted from the War Cabinet offices to Washington DC to arrange for seeds to be sent from America, and telephone calls made to Scotland and to the Ministry of Shipping, to arrange for seed potatoes to be provided and the necessary transport by sea to be made available.

Charles's task was to prepare propaganda material and to script training broadcasts to be transmitted to North Africa. His instructions were to prepare appropriate talks and to send copies to the War Cabinet.

One of his first acts was to telephone the North Africa Translation and Transmission Department of the BBC. To his amazement, the person who answered was none other than W.E. Proctor, whom Charles had known as a missionary with the North Africa Mission. Contact with him had been lost several years earlier, as Proctor had moved to Paris to work among the Moroccan community there. At the outbreak of war he had returned to London, where he had been recruited by the BBC.

It was just one of many strange meetings that happened in the war; when so many lives had been turned upside down, it was not surprising that some paths crossed in unexpected ways. Another extraordinary meeting took place when Charles was having problems with the Ministry of Information over the content of the broadcasts. He had used a biblical quotation ('Go to the ant, thou sluggard', Proverbs 6:6), and had emphasised, in the name of Allah and his word, that hard work was needed.

It was an approach he had used successfully in his missionary work; devout Moslems had a faith in Allah which was real and which provided a starting point for discussion. A telephone call from the Ministry of Information warned him to alter the script.

Charles requested an interview to explain why he had written the scripts in such a way. He was astonished and delighted to find, on entering the Chief's office, Sir Kenneth Grubb, with whom he had discussed non-professional missionary work back in 1925 and whom he had met again in 1935 in Madrid, at the first Protestant Congress ever allowed in Roman Catholic Spain.

'The trouble is that it will be seen as subversive propaganda,' explained Sir Kenneth, after the excitement of recognition was over. 'The Germans will say that we're trying to convert the Moroccans to the English Bible. It will be seen as an affront to Islam. It could set us back a long way. D'you think it's appropriate, in this sort of broadcast?'

Charles explained. 'I think it will go down very well with the Moroccans,' he said. Sir Kenneth's eyebrows lifted. 'You see, Solomon is one of their prophets as well. Proverbs is Solomon's book. They'll approve of the quote.'

The broadcasts went ahead, and soon the Moroccan farmers were listening to Charles's scripts, read in Arabic by three Arabs from the Moroccan Embassy in London:

The harvest has now started in earnest, and that which naturally springs to one's lips at this moment is the greeting I have so often heard and used during the many harvests I have been amongst you – 'Salaam Aleekoon – Allah Eekoon Fi Ilowan!'.

If the year is an early one, you will have just started the barley harvest. I have found that with many of you there is a great temptation to cut this too soon, as it is feared that if the weather is hot it will over-ripen and the grain will fall from the ear. Barley must not be cut until ripe . . .

The broadcasts continued for the next two years. Charles prepared seasonal agricultural and horticultural scripts dealing with sowing, care, harvesting, storage of various grain crops, crop rotation, and the growing of dozens of different vegetables. The talks included advice on the handling of dairy and beef stock, and on the management of vineyards, olive groves and the various types of citrus fruit trees.

THE BEGINNING OF THE END

The war years were not only times of danger, worry and work for the Fraser-Smiths. There were relaxed times as well, and time for holidays, making new friends, and spending time together as a family. The latter was even more important now; in the early years of the war their daughter, Christine, was born, and the family home at Croxley Green became noisy and full of laughter.

On Sundays, Charles and his family attended the local Brethren church. Life in the suburbs was rather less war-torn than in the city, but the area saw plenty of war damage. One Saturday night a land-mine was dropped on the church building in an air raid. Fortunately, alternative accommodation in the village hall was made available, but the original building stood unrepaired until after the war, when it was rebuilt elsewhere.

The end of the war, indeed, seemed to be drawing closer. Operation TORCH had been a great success, and Rommel's forces in North Africa had been driven back. Now the Allied Forces advanced into Europe and reached Paris. With the French capital once more in Allied hands, the work of supplying secret equipment to agents and

Resistance workers in Europe rapidly came to an end. But there were other theatres of war, and Charles's talents proved useful in supplying them as well.

He had already been involved in sending special secret equipment and concentrated rations to Orde Wingate and his Chindits in Burma, and supplies from MOS had been an important resource of the SOE agents there. But the supply situation in Burma was now a serious one. Goods which had been in store there, or had reached the Far East by long and complicated routes, proved to have withstood the delay badly. The heat, humidity and dampness wreaked havoc on metal and fabric. Vital spare parts, carefully stored, turned out to be rusted and corroded. Canvas webbing and fabric items sprouted lush growths of fungus and moss, eventually mildewing away. Paper and vital documentation wilted and decomposed in the sweltering damp heat. Armies of jungle insects and vermin also shared in the destruction. And despairing quartermasters realised that the nearest replacements were 6,000 miles away.

The situation was catastrophic for the war effort. Tanks and lorries that were vital for victory lay useless for lack of the right spare part, and as they lay idle they themselves began to deteriorate. Admiral Lord Louis Mountbatten sent an urgent message to the Anglo-American Packaging Committee:

> The soldier or airman in South East Asia is living and fighting in mountainous jungle country and under tropical conditions which cannot even be imagined by those of us who have lived only in temperate regions. Everything he possesses: his arms, his clothing, down to his bootlaces, remains wet for the greater part of the year and is under constant attack from mould and corrosion.
>
> It is absolutely vital that every type of equipment he is given should be able to withstand these conditions . . . . . Packing is equally important . . .

Such a serious problem demanded urgent attention. MOS commandeered the factory of Slazengers Ltd at Barnsley, and re-equipped it as a tropical packing factory, with the help of Slazengers' staff.[15] A rigorous programme was instituted, of cleaning items for despatch to the tropics, labelling them, and packing them in carefully selected materials, greaseproof paper, wax and bitumen.

The operation was an immense success, paying dividends for the remainder of the war with Japan, and the lessons learned were invaluable when supplying goods in the post-year wars to tropical countries in need of rehabilitation.

Charles's interest in Burma was more personal than just his experience of supplying secret equipment and directing a tropical packaging department. His brother Alfred, who was twice mentioned in despatches, served with the Royal Army Medical Corps with Wingate and Field-Marshal Viscount Slim, commander of the 14th Army in Burma. It was probably hearing his brother's stories of Wingate's character and deeply-held Christian faith that aroused in Charles a deep respect for Wingate and the 'Chindits' force that he created. Charles devoted a chapter to him in *Men of Faith in the Second World War* (1986).

By an odd coincidence, there was a young man in Burma at the same time as Alfred named Pip Fraser-Smith, who was no relation, and the duplication of names led to several postal mix-ups. Pip was in charge of SOE Burma, to which many of Charles's gadgets were sent.

He was a tall, fair-haired young man of twenty-two, with a very serious disposition for his age. He quickly acquired an MC by swimming a river in broad daylight under the noses of the Japs to steal a boat which he needed to get his men to safety. He had a very well hidden and secret HQ of his own, literally impossible to locate, near a little Naga village called Nanwunjang.

When the war in Burma ended, Alfred returned to his prewar work as a medical missionary in India with the Bible Churchmen's Missionary Society.

Charles himself had not abandoned Christian work in the pressures of war service, though he had to limit his interests to Crusaders, a work in which he had kept an interest since his late teens. Most Sunday afternoons throughout the war he was to be found in Rickmansworth, teaching his senior class of twenty boys. He considered it well worth the time spent in preparation and teaching, and he allowed almost nothing to prevent him from attending, even if he was on duty in London the same morning or evening and a long journey to the suburbs was involved.

Somebody else who took time out from an exhausting wartime schedule to help with the Crusader work was John Laing, who had shown such kindness to the Fraser-Smiths on their return to England. He often spoke to the boys at the Rickmansworth class, despite the massive programme of RAF airfield building in which he was engaged.

Afterwards he came to the Fraser-Smiths' home for tea, where he was an honoured guest: not only for the many Christian interests which he shared with Charles's family, but for his simplicity and warmth. When he sat in his favourite chair in the house at Rickmansworth, enjoying the view which rivalled that from his own home in Mill Hill, it was hard to remember that he was not only a very wealthy man, but also a great one.

Many of the boys who were Crusaders at Rickmansworth during the war years went on to devote their lives to Christian work. For example, a sixteen-year-old, John Lang, was a great help in the class and deputised for Charles on the rare occasions when he had to be absent. He later became Head of Religious Broadcasting at the BBC, and today is the Dean of Lichfield.

So Charles's life proceeded: a combination of a quiet family home in Croxley Green, with commitments in his local church and the local Bible class, and a job to be done in London that was of the greatest importance in maintaining supplies and equipment for some of the bravest and most vulnerable fighters of the war.

In writing of his war service afterwards, Charles described his own activities straightforwardly and, characteristically, directed the spotlight of publicity on the people he regarded as the real heroes and geniuses of the war: shop floor workers in British factories, working late hours to provide vital materials for CT6/MOS; Resistance workers risking everything to help escaping prisoners of war or to sabotage Nazi operations behind the enemy lines; great leaders such as Orde Wingate, Montgomery, Eisenhower, and Alanbrooke; and the hundreds of thousands of unsung men and women who fought on the battlefields and behind the scenes.

For Charles, the war meant a job of tremendous interest, with a great deal of job satisfaction. He did the job well: Alastair Macdonald, writing after the war in the Special Forces' Club newsletter, remarked of him,

> No reader can doubt how lucky we were that the drive, ingenuity and meticulous attention to detail of this remarkable man were made available in a field where the smallest imperfection was potentially disastrous.

But it was only an interlude. He was not a professional warmonger. Though he was to write several books later about his wartime experiences, he was fond of reminding his hearers and his readers that 'only fools and barbarians glorify war'. He regarded hostilities as a tragic necessity, a job that could not be shirked, which had to be done, and which had to be dealt with speedily and swiftly concluded.

One evening in May 1945 the end came. Charles had taken his briefcase into the bedroom for security. In it he happened to have a miniature radio set.[16] Sitting on the bed, he began to listen, turning the dial to find the latest news on the progress of the war.

So it was that he heard a clipped BBC voice announcing that hostilities in Europe were at an end – officially at one minute past midnight. General Jodl had made the final surrender of Germany to President Eisenhower near Rheims. The war was over.

CHAPTER NINE
Peace Returns

With the capitulation of Germany there remained only the
hostilities with Japan to be concluded. The end was not
long delayed. In August 1945 mankind crossed an
irreversible frontier: atomic bombs were detonated over
Hiroshima and Nagasaki. On 14 August, five days after
the Nagasaki explosion, Japan surrendered.

Charles's unique wartime task was now over. With the
end of hostilities, MOS turned to the necessary job of
organising the 'Prefab' Housing operation in readiness for
demobilisation and the homecoming troops. Charles was
involved in this enormous exercise, which required liaison
with local housing authorities all over Britain, and much
tedious paperwork.

Finding that this was not where his interests lay, he
obtained a transfer to a MOS department which was set
up for disposal of US Air Force equipment. The new job
brought him some unexpectedly glamorous assignments.
He had not been long behind his new desk when an urgent
request came for the loan of flying suits and various other
equipment; a film company was making a movie based on
a plane crash. Charles, having provided most of the
authentic props, was invited to watch the filming.

He inspected the film set approvingly, recognising the
skills of fellow gadget-makers. Artificial snow swirled
over the scene and piled in drifts against a life-sized mock-
up of the crashed airliner. As he watched, the cameras
whirred into action; the pilot smashed the window of the

cabin, shattering the artificial glass into realistic splinters, and clambered out, followed by the various actors playing the passengers. They included stars such as Margaret Lockwood and Denis Price, to whom Charles was introduced later.

The US surplus was stored at a large depot at Norton Fitzwarren, near Taunton. Another of the perks of Charles's new job was to eat at the Officers' Mess there. War rationing was still a gloomy necessity, but the American officers dined well, and so did their guests.

Early on in the new job, it looked as though introductions to famous film stars and gourmet lunches at the American base were destined to be an all-too brief interlude. The surplus material was transferred to aircraft hangars in Cornwall, and modern military equipment began arriving at Norton Fitzwarren. At the same time, Charles received secret instructions to be ready to return to his wartime work for MI6.

No reason was given for the mysterious order, and Charles did not expect one. He did, however, have his own opinions on the matter. It was his belief that holding MI6 in readiness, and restocking Norton Fitzwarren, were part of a plan by Churchill to maintain a top military profile in Europe, with the threat of direct action against an increasingly aggressive Stalin. Such a plan needed military supplies of the highest quality. Churchill, Charles reckoned, understood the European mind well, and had decided to maximise the areas of Britain's military superiority.

However, the order was not followed up, and Charles was not required to transfer back to MI6. It was bitterly frustrating for Charles; not because he would not now be returning to his war work, but because of the political implications. He deduced that America was reluctant to follow Churchill's lead, preferring to place her trust in 'the good faith of Marshal Stalin'.

In the postwar years he was often to return to the matter in discussion and point to what he took to be the consequences, as the sphere of Soviet influence overtook Korea, Vietnam and other parts of the world. In Devon, when the 'Cold War' was only a memory, he listened to three Poles working on his farm as they described their flight from Stalin's regime at the end of the war, and their conviction then that enslavement of Europe was the Soviet leader's dream.

In the meantime, the work of selling off surplus goods continued, and there were interesting visits to the Devon and Cornwall depots, often in the company of luminaries such as the Chief of MOS and the head of Marks and Spencers.

It was work well within the abilities of Charles Fraser-Smith, and he ran his office with the same meticulous precision that had characterised the 'Q' operation. The stocks of US surplus dwindled at a satisfying rate, and in due course a new job was offered him: this time, disposal of US surplus medical supplies.

It was an attractive proposition, and Charles took the job on; it offered long-term security. He was now set on the road to becoming a civil servant with a safe job. Work like that would always be needed, and he had shown himself to be good at it.

But the prospect of settling down behind a desk was not appealing. Charles had farmed the royal farms in Morocco and supplied gadgets to undercover agents all over Europe. He felt he had spent enough time as an army surplus shopkeeper. It was time to stir himself, to get back into the real world. Time, indeed, to return to what he regarded as the greatest enterprise on earth: obeying Jesus Christ's last and most important command, 'Go to all nations and spread the gospel.'

So he regarded his desk job with Medical Disposals as a strictly short-term arrangement. For him the future, he felt sure, lay elsewhere. With Blanche he considered, and prayed over, the various possibilities.

The most attractive was to return to Morocco, where,

if it had not been for the intervention of war, they would still have been living and working.

They considered going back to Sunset Farm. Though they had had little news of it during the war, Ben Khudda was still acting as manager and the farm was still a going concern. But perhaps farming there was no longer the only option. The long-delayed plans to establish an orphanage could still be put into action. They would teach the boys farming and horticulture, and the girls domestic skills; and, as in the prewar farming enterprises Charles had managed, there would be the influence of a Christian home and also systematic teaching about the Christian faith. Charles and Blanche were confident that in God's providence, a good number of the children would become Christians. In time those children would grow up and marry, and set up Christian homes in whatever part of Morocco they settled. And Ben Khudda, who had managed the farm while Charles and Blanche were doing orphanage work in Tangier and Marrakech, was a capable overseer of the day-to-day farming work.

British Government grants and reparations were available, and it was an easy matter to obtain permission to take enough money to Morocco to restock the farm and launch the new project. The Fraser-Smiths began to wind up their affairs in England, and prepared to say goodbye to their families and friends once again.

But their plans received a severe setback when, early in 1946, Charles developed medical problems. He was sent to University College Hospital in London, an enforced idleness which he accepted with characteristic ill-grace. He was far from being a model patient,[17] both because of his natural hatred of inactivity and because he was dismayed at the interruption to his plans for the new Morocco venture.

Worse was to follow. The treatment was successful, but Charles's doctors were very pessimistic about the Fraser-Smith's future plans. To move to Africa would invite health problems in the future; better for Charles to remain in England. Discussing the situation with Blanche, he realised he had no option but to accept the doctors' advice. They would have to abandon the orphanage plan.

Characteristically, Charles did not allow disappointment to stop him making other plans. The first need was to arrange the future of Sunset Farm, to which the Fraser-Smiths would not now be returning.

From his hospital bed, Charles made several telephone calls. He rang the Brethren magazine *Echoes of Service*, which was linked to hundreds of missionaries working throughout the world, and asked whether they would be able to take responsibility for the farm. They considered the proposal carefully, but decided that it was outside their current sphere of operations. Next he approached the North Africa Mission (today known as Arab World Ministries), but they too felt that the farm did not fit into any of their plans.

His next approach was by letter, to an American missionary society, the Gospel Missionary Union. This was a long-established society which had been working in Morocco for decades. The Swansons, who had given him hospitality and friendship when he first arrived in Khemisset, were missionaries with the society, and Charles had had considerable contact with its conferences and special meetings which the GMU organised in the region.

Having had two refusals, he was not over-optimistic. But he received a prompt reply expressing great interest. Not only was the GMU prepared to consider the proposal seriously, but they felt that everything seemed to point to them being the right organisation to take over Sunset Farm; especially the fact that during the war, the Americans had built an airfield near the farm, and Christian airmen serving there had expressed a desire to return to Morocco to work in missionary activities after the war. It was an obvious answer, and Charles and Blanche were sure that this was God's provision for the farm, and a clear indication that his plans for themselves did not include farming or orphanage work in Morocco.

Charles put the arrangements into the hands of Maître Henrion, a French notary in Morocco, and instructed him to draw up the necessary papers for sale at the price he had agreed with the Gospel Missionary Union. Then, conscious that a major problem had been resolved more satisfactorily than he had anticipated, he finally settled down to comparatively minor matter of convalescing.

He was in bed drowsing when a nurse came into the ward. 'Mr Fraser-Smith – a telephone call.'

An agitated voice crackled in the earpiece. 'It is Maître Henrion speaking. About the farm, the Khemisset property.'

'Is there a problem with the sale?' Charles resigned himself to long-distance problems and wished that he was more mobile.

'The sale, it is proceeding – that is straightforward.'

'Then what is the problem?'

'Your price. I cannot allow you to permit the sale at such a low price! Were you here in Morocco, you would know that the figure you have proposed is ridiculous. The farm has grown under your ownership. You have made an investment of time and money. You are entitled to a return on that investment and I, as your notary, cannot allow you to throw good money away. It is unprofessional! I would be defrauding you.'

'Please, Maître Henrion; allow me to speak.'

'No, Monsieur Fraser-Smith, listen to me. You bought my services in order to have competent professional advice, and it is my duty to give you that advice. Frankly, Monsieur, I believe you are being extremely foolish.'

'Maître Henrion, listen to me.' Charles took advantage of a momentary pause for breath in the outraged notary's tirade. 'The price will remain as I have decided.'

There was a snort of contempt at the other end of the line. 'Then I decline to act on your behalf.'

'Maître Henrion, the farm was bought as a missionary

enterprise. God's work has been done in that farm, and those who will own it now will also be doing God's work. Ought one to take a profit from doing God's work?'

There was a silence at the other end as the notary digested the argument. 'You will bankrupt yourself, nonetheless.' The notary sounded somewhat mollified.

'But I will not, Maître Henrion. The price I have negotiated with the Gospel Missionary Union ensures that I will receive from the sale the sum of my initial investment in the farm. That money, I will invest in England.'

Another long silence was ended by a resigned sigh. 'I will continue with the sale, Monsieur Fraser-Smith.'

The sale took some time, and Charles continued his work for the Ministry of Supply for the next year and a half. Though he was finding the work frustrating, it gave him the opportunity to consider his own future. There was an obvious possibility: to purchase a farm somewhere in Britain, and continue with his farming career. It was, after all, what he was trained to do, and his experiences in Morocco had confirmed that his approach to agriculture was enterprising and ingenious. Farming would give ample creative opportunities, and who knew what opportunities for Christian service the Lord might provide?

Charles and Blanche decided that this should be the next step. In 1948 the final papers were signed for the transfer of Sunset Farm to the Gospel Missionary Union, and the money from its sale was paid over to Charles, who promptly resigned from his work with MOS and began to look for a suitable property.

He looked at over fifty farms. All were either too expensive or in too poor shape. Having built his own house in Morocco, the prospect of getting a run-down farm into order was not a threat; but many farms in Britain needed more than energy. After five years of war, followed by post-war stringencies, they needed restocking and re-equipping. As he travelled and searched and prayed, he realised that his financial resources were not going to secure an early purchase.

Then a Christian estate agent contacted him.

'I've got a place on my books you might be interested in. Down in Devon. Two hundred and fifty acres – I'll take you down there.'

Aylescott Farm, at Burrington near Barnstaple, was in very poor condition. It was virtually derelict. Charles explored its 250 acres, gloomily noting the outbuildings in need of repair, the neglected fields, and the primitive farmhouse with its inadequate water supply and lack of electricity. If he were to bring his family to live in Aylescott farmhouse, what sort of an environment would it be for two children?

But he could see that the farm had potential, and his practised eye was already judging crops and yields, examining the good Devon pasture and various other natural advantages.

'Let's talk,' he said to the owner.

It was initially a disappointing conversation. The asking price was considerably higher than Charles could afford, even taking into account what would come in from the sale of their home in Rickmansworth and the money received from the GMU. Also money would be needed to restock the farm and to purchase equipment, feed and other necessities. And Charles had one or two ideas for the farm already in mind, which would need capital.

But as he and the owner talked, the possibility of purchasing the property became more realistic. The owner was selling because he wanted to retire, but was willing to leave his money invested in the farm for five years at a modest rate of interest.

That settled the matter. Charles and the owner shook hands, and Charles returned home with a favourable report to Blanche. The house in Rickmansworth was sold, and an overdraft arranged with the bank to finance a rapid restocking. The family moved to Devon in September 1948.

So began the next stage of Charles's life; set in the gentle hills of Devon rather than against the majestic backdrop of the Atlas Mountains, but similar in many ways to the days of pioneering in Morocco – and also, in its own way, as demanding of his ingenuity as his wartime work in MOS.

CHAPTER TEN
Aylescott

Before any farming could be started, the farmhouse had to be made habitable. When Blanche first saw the house which she was to turn into a home, caring for two children and performing the hundred and one tasks at which a farmer's wife needs to be expert, she was appalled. After the quiet comfort of suburban London, even in wartime, and the Moroccan farmhouse which had been fitted out with up-to-date equipment and furnishings, Aylescott farmhouse seemed squalid by comparison. But she began to put things to rights, and Charles turned his attention to improving the property.

The first essential was a proper water supply. The only domestic water available when they arrived was an ancient pump outside the back door, and the farm well was almost exhausted after a long, dry summer. Charles tinkered with the pump for half an hour and decided that it would be useless for their needs. He looked around for alternatives.

A quarter of a mile from the house, he found a clean stream. He constructed a small dam, and soon a pool of fresh water was available. Each day, he carried water across to the house in milk churns. It was a better arrangement than the pump and the dried-up well, but it was hardly a long-term solution, with winter on its way.

Exploring near the house, he noticed a patch of wet ground, and dug there. It turned out to be an underground spring. Having located a source of plentiful fresh water, it was a simple matter to install a pump and pipe

(i) Barcombe, Croxley Green. (pp.12ff)

(ii) Frank and Edith Piper.

(iv) Charles and Blanche
with Eric and Dorothy Fisk.
(pp.24ff, 47)

(iii) *Opposite* Charles, Blanche and
Brian at Khemisset in 1936. The
hedge shows three years' growth.
(Chapter 4)

(viii) *Opposite Above* A partner carries grain to the threshing floor.

(vi) *Opposite Below* The harvest tents and threshing floor.

(vii) Harvest Time. Charles and Blanche on horseback. (p.43)

(ix) Mint tea – outside a Berber tent.

(xi) Charles with a North African Christian and Mr Enyart of the G.M.U. (p.37)

Opposite Below Sheikh Ali, story teller and ballad singer. (p.46)

(xii) (xiii) North African teenagers in the thirties –
and in the sixties.

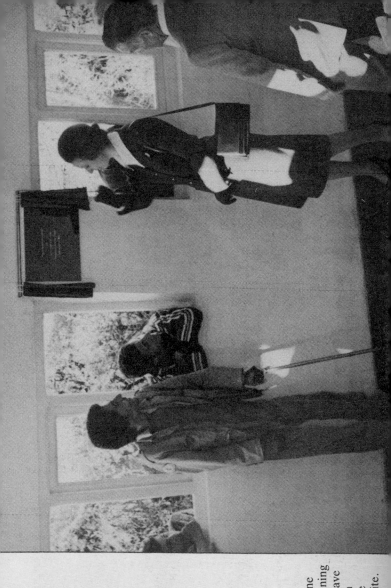

(xiv) HRH Princess Anne opens the dining hall at the Save the Children home on the Khemisset site.

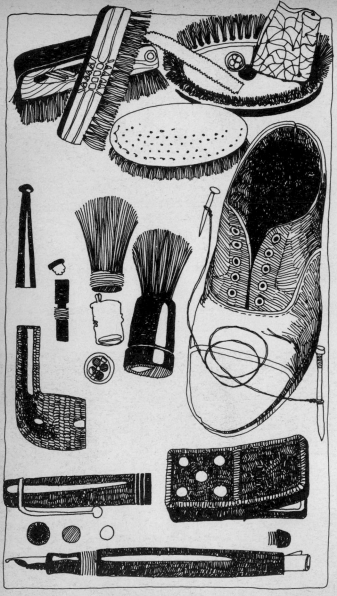

(xv) Pipes, pens, clothes brushes, dice, shoelaces and shaving brushes all concealed secret cavities and contents. The 'darning mushroom' was a landing light for aircraft. (Chapter 8)

(xvi) (xvii) Proofing and packing supplies for tropical use. (pp.82f)

(xviii) Slatted floors make it possible to collect the manure and wash it down the slope below for use as slurry. (The wire divisions were temporary.) (xix) *Below* Slurry is spread on the frozen ground ready for the thaw.

(xx) Charles with a 'Q' hair brush.

(xxi) *Opposite Above* With Desmond Llewelyn, who played 'Q' in James Bond films. (xxii) *Below* The office at Dale Cottage. (xxiii) *Above* Charles and Lin. (xxiv) *Below* Dale Cottage.

(xxv) Crusaders from a camp at Aylescott Farm visit Dale Cottage.

(xxvi) Keith Fraser-Smith directs the media branch of Arab World Ministries. (pp.173–183)

the water to a tank that Charles had placed in the roof of the house.

Yet, even with plentiful water, it was a hard winter. All cooking and lighting had to be done by paraffin, and the only lavatory was a two-seater in a shed ten yards down the garden path.

Gradually, matters improved, as a cooking range was installed in the kitchen, providing warmth as well as cooking facilities. But the family was without electricity for eighteen months, until Charles was able to purchase a second-hand generator.

His main interest was in beef farming, and with the help of a neighbouring Christian farmer, Charles Thomas of Umberleigh, he began to build up a herd of Devon cattle. He was genuinely fond of his cows, and gave each animal an Arabic name: *Ilzweena*, the Beautiful One; *Ilzoraha*, the Pearl; *Ilraghleeda*, the fat one.

It was some time before Charles was able to see whether or not he was making a profit. At first, the results were not encouraging.

'It's not working out,' he said abruptly to Blanche one night.

'What isn't?'

Charles was sitting at the kitchen table surrounded by bank statements, feed bills and farm accounts. 'The beef herd. It just isn't bringing in enough – not enough to cover the overdraft, the mortgage, the investment loan repayments, not to mention the children's clothes . . .'

'What can we do?' asked Blanche.

Charles looked at his figures again. 'We can expand into dairy farming,' he decided. 'That's where the money is at the moment. And we can't expand the farm with just a beef herd, anyway.'

There was no capital available to build large cowsheds and milking parlours to house a large herd, so Charles began to buy hardy Ayrshires, a tough breed that could winter out of doors without sheds.

The dairy herd was to be the key to expansion, fc
Charles had plans for the farm. He had pioneered farmin
methods in Morocco, and had discarded conventiona
ways of going about business in his work in MOS; now h
began intensive post-war pioneering on the farm i
Devon.

Within a week of deciding to start a dairy herd, Charle
invited down to Aylescott, one after the other, the to;
technical experts from three firms that were turning thei
efforts from making war equipment to manufacturin;
milking parlour equipment. He listened to what they had
to say, and decided to construct a milking parlour in which
one man could do the work of ten.

His experience in the war, of dealing with 300 firms
had taught him to identify the strengths and weaknesses
of different companies. With the aid of his three advisers,
and his own experience of farming in Africa, he devised
a system which was ahead of its time.

A problem he had experienced when he first learned to
shear sheep, for example, was back-ache. Trying to
straighten his back on the first day he had been unable to
stand upright. The solution then had been simple and
effective: dig a hole to stand in, and the sheep would be
at the right height for shearing without the need to bend
down. Now, designing his milking parlour, Charles
devised a system which allowed the herdsman to attach
the milking-machine clusters to the cows' udders without
having to bend.

The result was the first fully-equipped two-level milking
parlour in Britain. The idea quickly spread throughout the
country and abroad, and would no doubt have made
Charles rich had he had the time and inclination to protect
his idea and launch it commercially. But his time and
energies were committed to making the dairy herd
profitable. Blanche sometimes complained, only half in
jest, that Charles was giving priority to his modern and
progressive milking parlour, while she had to put up with

the inconvenience and frustrations of an old Devon farmhouse. But there was no alternative. Investing in the cows would pay the mortgage interest; but modernising the antiquated kitchen, redecorating the gloomy rooms and creating a pleasanter family environment were all things that had to come later.

The years that followed were hard, with working days of between twelve and fifteen hours. The children grew older. Brian, who had been a boarder at Monkton Combe School, was sixteen when they arrived at Aylescott, and when he left school he joined his father working on the farm. Christine spent most of her childhood on the farm, later attending Fernhill School in New Milton.

The family attended the Brethren chapel at Burrington, a small group of Christians meeting together, drawing their simple form of worship from New Testament patterns. Charles discovered, to his surprise and pleasure, that the chapel had been started a century earlier by George Muller, the founder of several large orphanages in Bristol. He had started the chapel in Burrington while on an extended holiday with a Christian farming family in the area. Thus, not for the first time, several areas of great importance to Charles were brought together.

The news from Sunset Farm was encouraging. For the first year of the GMU's ownership, three missionaries lived on the farm. At the end of the year they left, and in January 1949 Peter and Elsie Friesen married and moved to the farm. They were the first of many missionaries who lived and worked there, and the farm became the centre for Christian work that included North African Christian conferences, youth conferences, a major literature project, and the ongoing farming work.

The new work was not without problems. Ben Khudda, who had managed the farm since 1940, proved difficult to dislodge, and contested the GMU's right to the farm in the courts; even after a settlement was made by which part of the farm land was made over to him, he remained a problem. Yet even in that difficult relationship, there were opportunities to share the gospel and maintain a Christian witness. When Charles heard the story many years later, he confessed to feeling a good deal of admiration and affection for Ben Khudda, who had defended him several times in Morocco against local enemies and had managed the farm well during the Tangier orphanage project.

Overall, the work of Sunset Farm was developing very much as it would have done had Charles and Blanche been able to return; and that was a great encouragement to them. Though no orphanage was founded there, it became a venue for youth events; the farm was a constant witness to the local people in many ways (for example, a first-aid service was operated there); and lasting friendships were being forged between the missionaries and the Moroccan community, the strengths of which were to be demonstrated in the late 1960s when the situation of Christians in the region became very vulnerable.

Back in Devon, Charles was well into the programme of modernisation and innovation that was to make him, in the 1950s and 1960s, a notable figure in the British farming world.

Most of the land that Charles had bought was under 'old grass'; it had never been ploughed, and had not been treated with lime or fertiliser for twenty years. Most of it was incapable of yielding even a light hay crop. In his first year at the farm, Charles replaced the root crops, which had fed the cows in winter, with kale – a grazing crop which needed less manpower. He also abandoned hay-making, and switched to silage instead. In the following years he abandoned the accepted technique of giving one heavy application of fertiliser every year, in favour of several light dressings. In 1955, he gave up ploughing in favour of the rotovator, and also changed his pasturing method.

The results, particularly of the last change, were impressive. In 1957, the national magazine *Dairy Farmer* was able to report:

> Now the 160 effective acres carry 80 Ayrshires and 40 Red Polls; 45-50 cows are in milk all the year round, producing some 48,000 gallons of milk a year on a mainly grass and silage diet.[18]

How had the transformation been achieved? By putting into action Charles's deeply-held commitment to organic farming.

In the postwar years, the fashionable approach to pasture land management was 'ley farming', which was based on a mixture of various grasses and clovers, which was grazed intensively and then ploughed up when it reached the end of its useful life. The theory was that the goodness of the grass-clover mix, having provided nutrition for the herds, was then used to provide nutrition for the soil itself.

Charles was sceptical about this elementary approach to organic farming, and chose a different method at Aylescott. He put his fields under a permanent pasture, without clover, and farmed them intensively. He rejected hay-based management, and based his feeding strategy on silage. By the later 1950s, he was grazing his dairy herds for five months of the year on pasture alone, and the herd was still feeding from the fields up to January each year. Milk yields were consistently high, more cattle could be accommodated per acre, and Charles's herd was free of many common ailments, particularly bloat – a condition frequently found in grazing animals when feeding on lush pasture.

The success of permanent pasture techniques at Aylescott paradoxically brought about problems. When Charles bought the farm, part of the land was unworkable exhausted pasture. As he began to achieve results, he gradually brought more of the old pasture into use,

breaking up the old sward and re-sowing. What remained
was used as winter accommodation for the cattle. But as
more and more pasture was brought into full production
until by 1955 the farm was entirely permanent pasture, the
winter grazing given over to kale diminished. Before long,
the cows in winter had to be put on the permanent
pastures, which meant that twenty acres or so were
spoiled every winter.

This, combined with the awareness that 'wintering-out'
was not an ideal farming method even for the hardy
Ayrshires, made Charles reconsider the need for cowsheds. After several years of successful management the
farm finances were improving (as, indeed, was the
farmhouse!). Charles decided to erect a building.

A major difficulty was the cost of straw, which ruled
out the possibility of using conventional flooring. Alternative floors were available, such as cork and rubber, which
had the advantage that they could be merely hosed down,
thus saving time; but neither flooring interested Charles
enough to convince him that his new building should use
either of them. He put off starting to build while he
considered various flooring options.

It was ten years after Charles and Blanche had come to
Aylescott that a new trend in cowshed floors appeared;
slats, made of rails separated by a gap narrow enough to
avoid harming the cows' feet but wide enough to keep the
surface more or less dry.

The idea appealed to Charles, but characteristically he
improved upon it. The disadvantage of the system was
that dung, urine and spoiled feed collected underneath.
The slats had to be lifted, and the solids cleared out,
regularly. This was a lot of work.

He sketched out a plan: a series of low walls, three feet
apart, dividing the whole area into a system of narrow
canalisations sloping to one end of the building. The
channels were connected together at the bottom and
arrangements were made for water to be flushed into
them at the top. The diluted manure (or 'slurry' as it is

known in farming) would be allowed to escape into a central collecting area outside. The same system was used at the silage feeding face, in the calf and bull pens, perhaps even later an extension could be built to collect the water used for swilling down the milking parlour . . .. The slats would be laid across the low walls, providing dry flooring, and the warmth of the slurry below would be a decided bonus in the winter.

It seemed a foolproof plan, and Charles decided to investigate further. He applied for a Farm Improvement Grant, to provide the necessary funding.

The farm inspector was impressed by Charles's enterprise, but was nonplussed as to how to respond. 'I can't tell you whether it would work. I don't think anybody could tell you whether it would work. Nobody's ever tried anything like it before.'

'I know it will work,' Charles assured him. 'I've had a great deal of experience of irrigation methods in Africa. This is the same kind of thing. Believe me.'

'I reckon you probably could make it work,' the inspector conceded. 'But I tell you one thing. You'll never get a Farm Improvement Grant for a project like this.'

Charles digested the information in silence. The inspector hesitated.

'On the other hand,' he added, 'You certainly have a case for needing covered shelter for your cows. That will have a concrete floor. And you're eligible for a grant for a concrete area for your silage self-feed, too.'

Charles was awarded a grant to cover both needs, and soon he, Brian, his herdsman and tractorman, and a team of contractors, erected the new building. The main structure was erected by the contractors, but the design and construction of the concrete floor was done by Charles's staff under his supervision. The system was finished within a month. It worked perfectly.

The venture, combining labour-efficiency and high-yield organic fertiliser, rapidly produced impressive results. Meticulous as always, Charles paid special attention to the health factor; as nobody knew what diseases might build up on the oak wooden slats, he regularly scraped samples from them and sent them to a Christian friend, Dr Hobbs, at the National Health Laboratories in London, where they were tested for salmonella and other diseases.

News of Charles's pioneering scheme circulated locally and much further afield. He was interviewed and written about by the farming journals, and he wrote widely himself about the advantages of slurry farming. 'Probably the first system of its kind to be installed anywhere,' observed the *Farmer and Stock-Breeder*, a year after the building. 'And it works!'[19]

Experts and government dignitaries visited the farm: journalists, farmers and officials of the Ministry of Agriculture wanting to arrange demonstrations. European contacts were made, and Charles found himself travelling to explain his ideas overseas.

The story of the first decade at Aylescott makes impressive reading, especially when summed up as Charles summarised it in an article written in 1962, on the occasion of a Ministry of Agriculture visit to the farm. He looked back at ten years of eliminating costs, cutting out the obvious, and constant openness to new ideas. The results of these 'eliminations' he presented in a series of succinct, compelling statistics. Aylescott's milk yield per acre was 359 gallons; that of similar farms, 154. The figures showed a much higher utilisation of the soil resources, and each cow grazed a smaller acreage than cows in farms of similar size and situation.[20]

Farming colleagues were impressed and many adopted his ideas. He became well known as a controversial and compelling personality in farming. 'What pastures!' enthused T.H. Cooper in 1960. 'One hundred acres of them – leys, being left down as long as they are good, permanently if possible . . .'

Cooper concluded:

One can understand Mr. Fraser-Smith's enthusiasm for
what he feels is bound to be the next major development in dairy herd and grassland management – which
he and his son have pioneered.

'It is on men like him,' wrote another agricultural
journalist, 'that the future agricultural pattern of the
country will to a considerable extent depend.'
Yet another commentator summed up his achievements
even more succinctly, by dubbing him 'The Great High
Priest of Slurry'. Charles was pleased with the nickname,
though he always pretended to be rather unsure of
whether it was intended as a compliment or not.

CHAPTER ELEVEN
The Fighting Farmer

The photographs of Charles that accompany the magazine articles of the 1960s show a more relaxed person than the cool, rather enigmatic young man who looks out at you from the 1930s photograph reproduced on the cover of the paperback edition of Secret War. Of course he was older: in 1960 he was fifty-six years of age, and reaching a time of life when other men tend to begin to make plans for a quiet retirement.

But the Charles of 1960 was not interested in joining the ranks of the middle-aged. His life was lived in the hard work of the open fields and the cowsheds, in the happiness of his family home, and in the fellowship of his local church, and any one of the three would have given him ample opportunities for filling up a normal working life.

He was becoming a controversial figure, and he thrived on it. His personal copies of the articles written about him at that time are heavily underscored in ink with indignant exclamation marks and irascible retorts, as if he could not bear even to read a poor argument without reaching for his pen.

In his opinions he was often swimming against the tide. He argued passionately, for example, for a united Europe, at a time when the National Farmers' Union and the Ministry of Agriculture were deeply opposed to the idea. How could he argue otherwise, when he had been able to observe intimately the effect of a European war on individuals, homes and nations? To him, the French and Dutch farmers were not simply rival producers of produce. They were the labourers and housewives, the local officials and small traders who had been willing to risk everything to help the Resistance, the Maquis and the escaping British prisoners; people to whom he had sent gadgets, people whose names he hardly ever discovered. During the five years of the war, Charles had seen enough of a disunited Europe to convince him that the dream of a united Europe was a dream incomparably worth fighting for.

So he became an enthusiastic advocate of the EEC, and paid a price for it in some quarters, where he was seen to be jeopardising the welfare of his fellow-countrymen.

In 1958, Charles helped convene a large meeting in Exeter at which over 400 were present. The meeting was called because milk prices were poor and there was a threat of over-production. Feeling was strong, but the National Farmers' Union and the Ministry of Agriculture took no action.

A year later, Charles and some of his fellow-farmers met together in London, with a member of the Press, to consider forming an opposition group to current policies in the NFU, and the leadership of Sir James Turner. But they came to the conclusion that there was no point: the Union was committed to its policies, and opposition could mean disciplining by the NFU and consequent financial hardship.

In 1960, however, he began to use his pen to argue for milk quotas. Concerted action was urgently needed, he maintained, to reduce milk output to a rational level. Otherwise over-production would be inevitable, and food would be accumulated and spoiled. The National Farmers' Union was, again, opposed to the idea. It was a quarter of a century before the words 'butter mountain' became part of everyday language. But Charles's prophecy was correct. The butter mountains arrived, and the Common Market was forced to introduce milk quotas for member countries.

In 1960 he was also campaigning against pricing policies of the Ministry of Agriculture.

Have Price Reviews become a costly farce, are they out-of-date, are they not time wasters? Also could not all this vast energy and money, put into price reviews, be better diverted to things that bring immediate results such as group buying and selling (co-ordinated) and economic, controlled, production?[21]

His argument was that any formal Price Review structure by government inevitably kept prices low. What was also needed was an initiative by the ordinary farmer, negotiating direct with the suppliers.

Once again he found himself at loggerheads with the National Farmers' Union, to whom he had presented the proposal that a national farmers' co-operative be formed to enable bulk buying. The Union rejected the idea, and Charles became a founding member of an initiative by North Devon farmers who formed a group at South Molton under the leadership of John James. Brian Fraser-Smith was made a Director of the company. By negotiating with agricultural firms on the basis of a large group membership, they were able to negotiate substantial discounts – in some cases, goods were made available at half price. At the time of writing, the group is still thriving; now with 11,305 members, it covers a large area of Devon. The business is still transacted along the lines that Charles had a hand in determining at the outset; as little paperwork as possible, and a cash basis for all transactions. Any member defaulting on payment after fifteen days automatically loses membership.

There was great opposition to the scheme in the early days from the agricultural firms, who saw their profits jeopardised, and the co-operative received little or no support from the National Farmers' Union. Charles's part in the campaign was as a writer of articles and letters to the Press, and he received praise in some quarters and ridicule in others.

By the early 1960s the pioneering methods at Aylescott had begun to show some profit, and Charles's theory that such methods were the only way of generating a return on his investment was proving correct.

But the effects of the war on the national farming economy had made it a slow struggle, and even now there was no prospect of resting on his achievements.

It was true that the farmhouse was now a comfortable family home, unrecognisable from the building they had taken over in 1948. Also the children had both attended good schools; and now Brian was playing an increasingly important part in the farm and becoming a well-known local agriculturalist in his own right, and Christine was launching out on a nursing career at the Middlesex Hospital.

But Charles foresaw lean times ahead in British dairy farming, and was convinced that the only way to survive was to maximise the efficiency of every aspect of farming. Following his programme of 'eliminations', he now turned his attention to the 10,000 yards of earth banks and dilapidated hedgerows that his property contained. In 1962 he once again became a figure of controversy when he bulldozed all internal hedgerows on the farm and erected high-tensile fences, on the Australian pattern, in their place.

The conservationists hated him for it, but Charles stuck to his guns.

He was accused of depriving animals of natural shelter; he replied that a cow's instinct, in a field without trees or other shelter, would lead it to seek parts of the field that had cool air currents or less wind. Besides, a cow that was in discomfort from bad weather could make its own way to the warmth of the cowsheds by the internal road and gate system Charles had made on the farm.

Others accused him of wanting a sterile, bleak

environment, where all natural beauty had been sacrificed for the benefit of a dehumanised efficiency and profit motive. Charles responded by pointing out the belt of trees and shrubbery across the property, providing shelter for bird life and also justifying their existence on aesthetic grounds – even though they used up valuable acres with no commercial return whatsoever.

There was opposition also from those who deplored the loss of natural hedgerows. This is perhaps the aspect that would arouse most antagonism today, when miles of historic hedgerows are being uprooted every year to maximise agricultural profit, and conservationists have a valuable role as protesters against unthinking and uncaring damage to the environment.

But the hedgerows at Aylescott were not historic ones, representing generations of growth and a long-established ecology. They were a legacy of the years of neglect and poor management that Charles had inherited. The hedges, often little more than a straggle of unkempt thickets along a soil bank, were recent plantings: they were space-consuming, time-consuming to maintain, and in addition robbed the soil of food for some yards on either side.

The scheme met with a mixed reception. When Charles wrote about it in the farming press, the editor prefixed the article with a note to the reader:

> We do not endorse the view of the author . . . In our view it is essential that shelter belts are available for cattle in all fields.[22]

(Charles agrees that shelter belts in certain areas following correct contour lines may have their place. But he contends that earthbanks and hedges are purely man-made barriers erected for rotational grazing small herds of stock, and they have many disadvantages known to experienced farmers.)

The elimination of hedgerows was part of a vision Charles had for the future of dairy farming:

> This leads us to consider what I maintain will be the economic dairy farm of the future, of 200 intensive acres and with over 200 head of stock, run by the farmer and one man, with help only at the time of fodder or silage harvest.[23]

It was not a utopian dream. He had demonstrated its viability at Aylescott, and he had also been able to obtain comparative figures from analysis of his own results using slurry and intensive dairy farming, and more conventional methods. They demonstrated that the nutrient value of slurry far exceeded that of other organic fertilisers.

It might have seemed that Charles was in his element. Always a pioneer, he was now a campaigner against the tide; and his ideas were not just agricultural reforms. He never separated out his concern for the soil from his concern for the world as a whole. Issues of world peace, use of resources, tolerance, and a determination never again to repeat the waste and tragedy of two world wars, surface in all his writings of the period. The conservationists who attacked him for uprooting hedgerows would have been nonplussed to read his later proposals to reclaim the Sahara desert; but it was not an about-face.

Charles had great ideals to fight for, and great vision. His experimental farm was the testbed for new methods which were to have repercussions nationally and internationally. There was no reason why he should not spend the next ten years refining his techniques and advocating his beliefs.

No reason at all. But a shadow was to fall across the Fraser-Smiths' lives that would change everything.

CHAPTER TWELVE
The Valley of the Shadow

In 1963, Blanche, who had not been well for some time, underwent medical tests. The results shattered the orderly routine of life at Aylescott. Blanche was diagnosed as having developed leukaemia.

The prognosis was as bad it could be: she was not expected to live for longer than six months. The Fraser-Smiths' life took a new and sombre direction.

One of the first decisions that the family made was that the bustle and constant telephone-ringing of modern intensive farming, especially that of a large dairy farm working a seven-day week, would be intolerable for a woman with a debilitating illness.

The decision to leave the farm would have been appallingly difficult in any other circumstances; there was so much planned that had not yet been begun, so many projects half-completed. But, not for the first time in their lives, Charles and Blanche abandoned the plans they had made and stepped forward into an unknown and troubled future, trusting in God to show them what to do next. They found a house in nearby Barnstaple without difficulty, and moved in. Charles formally handed the farm over to Brian, who was by then 32 years old and soon to be married.

Blanche's treatment involved heavy doses of drugs, which a consultant from Exeter administered at the beginning of each new wave of pain. After each treatment, three weeks of mental deadness followed, after which she was well for a further three weeks before the onset of another attack.

It was a harrowing experience for Charles as well as Blanche, and he asked to see the consultant who had prescribed the treatment. He wanted to know whether the severity of the treatment was intended to cure her, or even prolong her life. On receiving the answer that it could not be expected to achieve either purpose, Charles insisted on stopping the treatment. Instead, he requested that the drugs be given every day in small doses. The result was that she was mentally alert all the time, and lived for two years instead of the predicted six months. Under the new regime, she enjoyed a very good quality of life. She was able to go out in the car until the last stages of her illness, enjoying the beauty of the Devon countryside.

They decided to leave the Brethren chapel at Burrington and find a church near at hand, so that Blanche could have fellowship locally. In Barnstaple they found a welcome among Brethren there. Their decision to join the fellowship at Grosvenor Street Chapel was confirmed for them by yet another of the delightful 'coincidences' that recurred in their daily lives: the chapel had been founded, over a hundred years before, by Robert Cleaver Chapman, who had been the young Charles's hero and had prayed with Edith Piper, Charles's guardian, on the eve of her departure for missionary service in Spain.

Indeed, it seemed that at this distraught time in their lives, God was giving them many signs of his presence and care. Such a sign concerned Morocco, which was never far from their thoughts, even though Sunset Farm was now in the capable hands of the Gospel Missionary Union. About eighteen months after the initial diagnosis, as had happened so often before, God brought into Charles's and Blanche's life a new reminder of the country and of an old friend.

It came about through the Barnstaple and District branch of the British and Foreign Bible Society. Blanche's excellent response to the new treatment meant that she was able to take over the leadership of the women's section, and Charles joined the general committee at the same time, going on to become the Chairman and eventually President (in 1973, he was made an honorary life governor of the Society).

A colleague on the committee, Mrs Keevil, remarked one day, 'I think there's a project that will interest you. A new Moroccan Arabic translation of the Scriptures.'

Charles was immediately intrigued, and asked for more details.

'It's being done by a Captain Fisk,' she said. 'He's looking for financial help to publish it.'

Charles was delighted to have news of Eric Fisk, who had begun his mammoth translation task in 1952, when there was a danger that the missionaries would be expelled from Morocco; if that were to happen, Fisk decided, it would be essential that the Moroccans had the whole of the Bible in their own language.

He arranged a week of meetings for Fisk in North Devon, and introduced him to a number of influential people. The Captain's military bearing and compelling speaking style aroused great interest, and the visit played a major part in financing the Moroccan Bible project. Generous help was also given by Sir John Laing, who had received his knighthood in 1959, and who later also helped with the funding of Fisk's Moroccan colleagues in the translation work.

Eric Fisk's visit was a wonderful opportunity to share reminiscences of the work in Morocco, and to exchange news gleaned from Moroccan contacts. It was a visit touched with a great deal of sadness, for nobody knew how long Blanche might live; but it brought joy as well.

Not long after Fisk had left, Charles desperately needed a break. He was almost exhausted from his constant and devoted nursing of Blanche. So they discussed the problem, and decided together that Charles ought to take a short holiday. Their daughter Christine, who was nursing in London at the Middlesex Hospital, came down to Barnstaple to take over from Charles for a fortnight.

Charles took the farm mini-van, packed it with enough food and other necessities to enable him to eat and sleep in the van, and set off for a touring holiday on the continent.

A steady stream of postcards and letters home recorded Charles's impressions of a countryside not unlike that of Devon, as he drove through Brittany and Normandy. The residents' natural, leisurely life appealed to him. He saw women carrying pails on yokes, and wearing wooden sabots on their feet as generations of French peasants had done before them. It was a region that was very important to him, full of memories of brave men and women whose lives had briefly touched his own in the war.

Then he headed south to Bolléne, in a dry, arid area of France which he particularly wanted to see. When Morocco had gained its independence, French farmers there returned to France. Many of those coming to Bolléne had gained experience of irrigation techniques on the southern edge of the Atlas Mountains, bordering the Ṣahara. The needs of a rapidly developing farming community were being met by major canalisation projects and hydroelectric power stations.

His road to Switzerland took him through Grenoble and the Mont Blanc tunnel. He was the guest of the Swiss Director of Agriculture, one of the Europeans who had written to him when his innovative farming techniques began to attract international attention.

The Director insisted on hearing all about Charles's pioneering slatted-floor slurry techniques that he had developed in Devon. He was asked for his advice on a dairy project which was being constructed by prisoners at a new reformatory. The Swiss authorities had taken over 1,000 acres of swampy ground, and the prisoners had drained it and were beginning to farm it.

Charles was asked to suggest an appropriate slatted-floor system for the new dairy herd. He found it extraordinary to be talking to men and women who included murderers, even though most of their crimes had been murders of provocation or accidental manslaughter.

He drove back through Germany, through the Black Forest and on into France, finally taking a night boat to Southampton after spending a day at Honfleur, the idyllic fishing port which had been a haven for the impressionist painters and still looks today as picturesque as it had when its famous visitors stayed there. Among memories of the fortnight was a visit to Dinard on the south coast of Brittany, where the world's first tidal power station had been built. Charles was, characteristically, fascinated by it, and sent an enthusiastic postcard home to Blanche.

He returned to Devon refreshed. Over the next months he and Blanche held several Bible Society meetings in their home, and at one of them she gave a talk to the women's committee, in the form of a Bible Study on Ephesians 6:10-18. The notes for that talk are reproduced in *Four Thousand Year War*.[24] She began with a comparison which echoed much of Charles's past and future writing:

An army is never sent to war inadequately equipped. In history any such army suffered defeat. We have been called and chosen for his service, and he sends us out to fight his battles, that is, to stand against the forces of evil which are against us but he has provided very adequate equipment or armour for us to meet the enemy. Do we avail ourselves of it or do we endeavour to stand in our own strength?

Her own strength was declining rapidly. A few days later she was drowsy for much of the day, but at eleven o'clock in the evening she suddenly said that she would like a game of Scrabble. She played well, and beat Charles, which was something that rarely happened. At one o'clock that morning, she died.

In 1963, when she was first suffering the symptoms of leukaemia, Blanche had written these notes on the flyleaf of her Bible:

'Casting down *imaginations* . . . and bringing into captivity *every* thought to the obedience of Christ' (2 Cor. 10:5).

'For God hath not given us the *spirit* of *fear*, but of *power* and of *love*, and of a *sound mind*' (2 Tim. 1:7).

Remember the Edelweiss grows on rocky mountain heights – its soft beauty is a cheery surprise to the toiling climber.

Her funeral was conducted by Albert Fallaize, at whose home in Morocco she and Charles had spent happy holidays.

It had been a wearying three years for Charles nursing Blanche. Apart from the brief holiday in Europe, he had had no break. With his task over and the farm flourishing under Brian's management, now was the time to consider revisiting Morocco. Within three weeks he was there.

His decision was dictated by several factors. Of course, he looked forward to seeing the country again and meeting old friends. His wartime broadcasts had produced many contacts which he wanted to follow up. But an idea was filling his head, another pioneering Fraser-Smith scheme: he wanted to start a mobile Bible and literature shop.

The war in North Africa was over, but a new war had begun and was raging fiercely. Communist interests had tried to turn Islam to its advantage by sending Soviet-trained Moslems, but they had little success, and the Communists turned to the written word.

In the early days of missionary work, there were few translations of Christian books available, and fewer literate Arabs who could read them. There was no complete Moroccan Arabic Bible, until Eric Fisk began

his great work of translation in 1952. But the world was
now fast becoming literate. The power of the media was
well understood, and radio and written material could
penetrate where missionaries could not go.

It was essential to grasp the opportunities before
Communist and other anti-Christian interests gained a
monopoly. Thus Charles envisaged mobile literature units
in North Africa – and also in France, where increasing
numbers of North Africans were flocking to find work.
Full of enthusiasm for the idea, and looking for a new
interest, Charles set out for North Africa.

Travelling in Morocco during the winter of 1965-66, it
was impossible not to notice the changes. Moroccan
Islamic anger at the actions of the French dating from
1930, when a concerted attempt had been made to
influence the large Berber tribes away from Islamic
loyalty, had resulted in the founding in 1943 of *Istiqlal* –
the Independent Party. Later it became the Freedom
Movement, and ten years later the puppet Sultan,
Mohammed V, gave his full support to it. He was
deported to Madagascar, and his uncle, Arafa, was made
Sultan in his place, though it was not a role which he
sought. This only made matters worse, and in 1955
Mohammed was brought back. The following year,
Morocco gained her independence.

Postwar Morocco was thus a very different place from
the country that Charles had known. He had seen
Mohammed V become Sultan in 1927, and had seen the
beginnings of unrest as the French paid subsidies for the
building of Roman Catholic churches. One had been built
at Khemisset, and dedicated to Saint Theresa and the
infant Jesus. It was all part of an attempt to reduce Islamic
power in this Berber region, so that with the reduction of
power would come the gradual dismantling of a fanatical
Islamic way of life.

However, within six years of Independence, an Islamic
religious intolerance reigned in Morocco. A new penal
code was introduced. Influencing a Moslem into abandon-

ing Islam was now an offence punishable by three years' imprisonment. The offence covered exploiting a weak Moslem's vulnerability, or using 'institutions of education, health or orphanages'. (Today, it is illegal for a Moslem to change his faith.)

The missionaries and the Christian community were now living in very difficult circumstances. Shortly after arriving in Morocco, Charles read the Moroccan newspaper *Maghareb Al' Arabi*, and encountered a savage attack on Christian literature distributed by missionaries or sold in their shops. It was the worst of poisons, said the newspaper, and announced that the newspaper was opposed to the 'neo-colonialist intellectual infiltration' which showed itself in foreign religious missions and their missionaries who came to sow error. Other targets of the criticism were the Christian camps held at Sunset Farm, Khemisset and elsewhere in Morocco.

Charles spent a few days in Tangier with Eric Fisk. He had closed down his Christian work at Tabahounite since Independence Day, and was now working hard to finish his translation work in order to leave behind the whole Bible in Arabic suitable for Morocco and all North Africa.

In Casablanca, Charles was fascinated to see the new government's emphasis on education and even physical training. Young girls as well as young men were drafted into training programmes.

At Khemisset, Charles spent fifteen days on Sunset Farm and rejoiced to see the new buildings housing the printing press and the distribution of the Bible Correspondence Course begun by the Gospel Missionary Union.

At Marrakech, there was a reunion with his old partner Bryce Nairn and his wife Margaret. They had had a remarkable life since the prewar farming days. Just before the war Bryce had joined the Foreign Office, and became Consul at Marrakech. When Churchill visited there, it was Nairn who looked after him, and Margaret Nairn painted with Churchill on several occasions. In 1944, Churchill's wife wrote to her daughter:

> There is a very nice British Consul here [at Marrakech],
> Mr Nairn. He and his wife are both Scots. I like them
> both very much. She is an artist.

Among other well-known people who crossed the Nairn's
path during the war years were the De Gaulles, Duff and
Diana Cooper, and Max Beaverbrook. In 1966, when
Charles revisited Morocco, they were retired, Bryce
having completed his years in the diplomatic service as
Consul General in Tangier.

From Marrakech he crossed the Atlas Mountains to
Ouarzazate on the edge of the Sahara, where Kaye
Richmond ran an independent medical and midwifery
work. It was known as the Dades Valley Fellowship, and
later joined up with Arab World Ministries.

The old days of Morocco had gone for ever. The war had
opened up new means of production and had forced an
efficiency on a workforce which had previously been
conspicuous by a charming laziness. At Agadir, Charles
was taken into the upland region by the Moroccan Head
of Forestry and shown the extensive redevelopment that
was taking place. Numerous small schools had opened,
where elementary education was available. Charles
looked round a few of them. The curriculum was
prominently displayed on the wall. One of the subjects
taught was the difference between Islam and Christianity.

Looking at the landscape, Charles remarked 'I gather
that the French built the magnificent roads we've been
travelling on.'

The Forestry Official shook his head. 'We did the
work,' he said emphatically. 'Every man had to give ten
days' free labour every year. The people built the roads.'

Later, travelling in a valley leading into the Atlas
Mountains, he discovered a gracious house and garden
belonging to a Moroccan architect and sculptor, who
invited him to look around the garden. In the garden was
one of the sculptor's statues: a beautiful woman, kneeling

in an attitude of prayer and worship. Charles recognised the statue.

'That statue of *Mariamma* (Mary) is wonderfully correct,' he said. 'I know well that Islam accepts Mary as the mother of Jesus the Prophet, and that in your faith she is said to be a virgin. And in the *Injeel* (Gospels) we see Mary worshipping like that, saying "My soul doth magnify the Lord." You certainly understand our New Testament teaching about Mary better than many Europeans who make statues of her and pray to them. Here you have shown Mary herself in prayer.'

The sculptor nodded gravely. 'I have seen much idolatry among your Europeans,' he agreed. 'Many magnify Mary, not the Jesus of the *Injeel*. They make her into a goddess, and do not follow their Holy Book. They make images, and break the commandment of God: "You shall not make any graven image or any likeness and bow down to them."'

It was a sobering encounter. Charles felt the need to gather together his many impressions gained during the trip. The Morocco of the 1960s was very different from the Morocco he had known and farmed in his twenties. New religious battles were being fought, and secular Communism was striving to gain the hearts of men and women.

What was the role of the Christian church in all this? How could British Christians help? And how best could the resources of Moroccan missions, already stretched unbearably, be deployed in this new situation?

He went back to the house he had built for himself and Blanche in Khemisset. There he was looked after generously by the Peabodys, a couple who were living in the house and working for the Gospel Missionary Union literature operation. From Charles's description of the visit in letters he wrote later, it seems that in that place which was full of memories for him they helped him begin to come to terms with his grief.

With their help he drew up a two-page summary of his impressions.[25]

It was a document which was to guide his thoughts and his work for North African missions for the rest of his life. Like so many enterprises which Charles had founded, it was a pioneering gesture. He defined the aim of missionary work as 'forming churches', and emphasised the need for mobile resources. He pointed to the scarcity of truly indigenous North African churches. And he conceded that the door to missionary work in North Africa was almost closed.

But he proposed a radical missionary thrust: that resources and energies be devoted to the millions of Arabs in Europe, to evangelising the Arab student world, and to reaching the new generation of Arabs. He was advocating pulling out Christian involvement in Morocco, and redeploying in Europe. And he issued an appeal for the formation of mobile literature units and a renewed initiative in Christian literature.

Sadly, the scheme proved unworkable. The capital sums required were too high, and the resources of the missionary societies of the time too low. Most missionaries in the field were struggling to make ends meet, and it was not possible to divert non-existent funds to underwrite a new and untried project.

But the document, in many ways, foreshadowed much later academic thinking about mission. And it clarified Charles's thinking and confirmed his various impressions formed during the trip. After the temporary diversion of the war, Charles Fraser-Smith's commitment to his beloved Morocco and the Moroccan people was as strong as it had ever been.

CHAPTER THIRTEEN
New Directions

Charles returned to England with a renewed burden for missionary work, and a conviction that the war had produced a transformed Europe and Africa, demanding that old assumptions be discarded and new ways of thinking be devised to confront the shattered empires and new alliances left by the conflict.

God's timing, a constant wonder in Charles's action-packed life, was demonstrated once again when on a visit to Louth in Lincolnshire he met Selina Richardson, known to everybody as Lin. Lin Richardson's family connections extended back to Archbishop Stephen Langton, who influenced the drafting of Magna Carta,[26] and to John Tillotson, a widely-read preacher of the seventeenth century who was Archbishop of Canterbury 1691-94.

Her mother, Marjory Tillotson, had in 1908 become designer for J. & J. Baldwin of Halifax, who published the first knitting-patterns ever seen in Britain outside ladies' magazines; and Lin ran her business under the same name.[27] She was a fashion knitwear designer, whose customers included several of the Queen's ladies-in-waiting.

Charles and Lin had interests in common and several family links – Lin's cousin, for example, had been at Brighton College when Charles had been a boy there. Over the next six months their friendship grew into something stronger: and in September 1966 they realised that God was calling them into marriage.

Lin's business training and infectious enthusiasm complemented Charles's plans and visions for the future. He developed a renewed interest in the Common Market, which he had defended in articles in farming journals for some time, standing against the declared opinion of Sir James Turner, the President of the National Farmers' Union. It seemed transparently logical to Charles that a Europe united economically and politically, strong enough to resist any world power wanting to dominate it militarily or economically, was far preferable to the maiming and killing that had soaked Europe in blood twice in his adult lifetime.

The theme of arming for security runs through all Charles's writings. In his books he frequently refers to such Bible verses as Luke 11:21 – 'When a strong man, fully armed, guards his own house, his possessions are safe.' He looked pessimistically on what he regarded as appeasement in the early postwar period, and linked twentieth-century wars with the words of Christ that 'nation will rise against nation, and kingdom against kingdom' (Matt. 24:7).

To some readers this emphasis has probably seemed war-mongering, but it is a misleading interpretation. For Charles, war is the hated last resort, the calamity which is brought about by weakness and lack of preparation.

His interests extended beyond war-battered Europe, to Africa. In 1969 he became interested in Botswana, a country experiencing similar problems to those of Morocco: low surface water, extensive desert areas in the Kalahari to the South, and swampy delta land in the Northwest, similar to that which he had seen in France, with great possibilities for agricultural development. He used his Bible Society connections to attempt to interest the United Nations in a Bible distribution project for Botswana. The United Nations Association is an organisation working among the public and among schoolchildren to promote the work of the U.N. Its Western Regional Council was active in sponsoring working projects in

Botswana, and Charles pressed vigorously for educational initiatives and Bible distribution to 'feed the minds'.

The U.N. did not respond to the Bible proposal, and nothing came of it, except the opportunity for Charles to correspond and exchange ideas with Jim Legge, a missionary in Botswana working in fellowship with *Echoes of Service*.

The United Nations Association was at that time campaigning for 100,000 members. A particular thrust in the campaign was towards the young, which Charles, who always numbered young people among his many friends, approved of. He was also disturbed at the criticism that was expressed of the United Nations in many quarters: while he readily conceded its faults, he felt that the scale of international co-operation it represented, and the number of projects involved, demanded support. Charles regarded it as the duty of everybody to work in some way to bring harmony to the world: a duty which he felt rested particularly upon Christians.

The interest in Botswana brought Charles into close contact with the United Nations Association in Devon, and soon he was approached by the Barnstaple and District branch. They needed a secretary urgently; was Charles interested?

He accepted the job on a temporary basis, and remained as secretary for two years.

He plunged into the work enthusiastically, speaking in schools and various other venues all over Devon. His slogan 'Unite or be atomised' was reported several times in the Press, and his slides of the Sahara Desert, the Atlas Mountains, and numerous cameos of Moroccan life were enjoyed by many audiences as he spoke in support of UNICEF (United Nations Children's Fund) and the Save the Children Fund.

'This fund,' he announced in a newspaper interview, on a UNICEF flag day, 'is working to ensure that every child has and enjoys the basic rights to which every human being is entitled.'

Charles's internationalist interests were appropriate, for the situation in Morocco had deteriorated sharply so far as Christian work was concerned. In the 1960s, the work at Sunset Farm had grown tremendously. There had been difficulties and sadnesses; Elsie Friesen, who had begun the work there in 1948 just after her marriage to Peter, died at Sunset Farm, and two years afterwards the Friesens' six-year old son, Virgil, also died. Another missionary couple working at the farm, the Barcuses, were bereaved of a child. But God had blessed the work that was going on. By 1969 accommodation for at least a hundred people had been erected, over five thousand eucalyptus trees had been planted, a swimming pool had been built, and the well and water system had been greatly improved.

It seemed that the work was going from strength to strength. But as the political situation changed, and the Islamic regime introduced increasingly stringent controls on Christian work, the Gospel Missionary Union realised that their days in Morocco were numbered. In 1969 their fears were realised. Most Christian missionaries working in the country were requested to leave.

In England, Charles heard the news of the expulsion of the missionaries with distress, though he had anticipated some such eventuality, as had Eric Fisk when he began his translation work in 1952. It seemed that many hopes and prayers had come to nothing, as Sunset Farm stood empty again, with all the missionaries gone.

But in 1972 Charles heard with great joy that the Gospel Missionary Union had negotiated with the Save the Children Fund to allow them to rent the farm for their work in Morocco. To the farm now came handicapped children, polio victims, and crippled children from poor families. There they received expert orthopaedic help and medical supervision, and were then encouraged to do as much as possible for themselves: many enjoyed climbing frames, rope climbs, football and hopscotch.

At the farm they received an education. Many left to

go on to university. It was work which Charles had already been supporting by his work for UNICEF and Save the Children Fund, and it was a miracle that the farm had been taken over by an organisation for which Charles and Lin shared a close affection. They were thrilled to know that most children who grew up at the farm, having overcome major handicap, were able to go out and lead happy, useful and normal lives. Although the work at the farm was now directed at children's physical welfare only, Charles and Lin knew that the work done by generations of missionaries in Morocco had born fruit and would bear fruit in the future. In the meantime, the farm was in good hands.

And the story of the farm continues. As this book went to the printer, Captain Mark Phillips, the husband of the Princess Royal, visited Barnstaple on an official engagement, and Charles was able to spend some time in conversation with him. Captain Phillips was interested to hear about the progress of the work since the Princess Royal had visited Sunset Farm in 1984, and about the plans of Captain Robert Hayward of the Officers' Christian Union to open a second Save the Children Centre near Marrakech, run on similar lines.

Charles was also able to report the achievements of a handicapped girl who had been equipped with artifical arms sent out from England. She had become an enthusiastic student of English, had gone to England where she had gained a degree in English, and has since obtained a position with the BBC in London.

CHAPTER FOURTEEN
A Hungry World

In 1973, Charles was in his sixty-ninth year. His interests were as wide-ranging as ever. He was doing more writing: his meticulous mind found the organisation of ideas easy, and his experience in Morocco, presenting the gospel to highly sophisticated Muslim minds and uneducated farm labourers alike, had trained him in the art of getting his point across. The wartime radio scripts directed to Moroccan farmers had shown him at his best: an easy familiarity with the everyday realities of how the people lived, coupled with an assured authority which often characterises the expatriate Englishman abroad who finds himself in a management situation.

Now, with new ideas and causes to champion, he kept his pen busy. His involvement with the United Nations Association, UNICEF and the Save the Children Fund had made him sharply aware of the increasing problems of the Third World and world hunger.

In the early summer of 1973, the editor of the Open Brethren magazine *The Harvester* sent him a copy of an article which was due to be printed in the July issue. 'A Christian contribution to the Third World' was written by Dr H.S. Darling, Principal of Wye College in Kent, London University's School of Agriculture and Horticulture. Darling provided a thoughtful discussion of rural development projects in underdeveloped countries, and it was clear from the opening paragraph that his approach to missionary work was very close to that of Charles and Bryce Nairn on their arrival in Morocco.

. . . It is not surprising that missionary societies are
becoming increasingly conscious of the need to be
involved in rural development projects to increase the
effectiveness of their spiritual witness in the under-
privileged communities to which they have been called
to serve. Such involvement can be a means of much
blessing to all concerned. Not only does it bring the
missionary into close and sympathetic contact with
those to whom he wishes to preach Christ, but it also
affords him many splendid opportunities for helping
them to help themselves in a way calculated to ensure
a willing and friendly hearing for the Gospel message.

Darling advocated investment in education, training,
community development and intermediate technology.
His analysis was objective and honest:

An important aspect of the situation is that through
devotion to medical and educational work the missionary societies have unwittingly aggravated the difficulties
by increasing the population of unemployed school-
leavers. Is it too much to hope that the agricultural
missionary will redress the balance?[28]

Roy Coad, the editor of the *Harvester*, asked Charles
for comments to be published in a later edition. Charles's
article, 'Save our S. . .?', appeared in the September
issue, warmly appreciative, as may be imagined, of
Darling's arguments.

Two years later he was in contact with Dr Darling
again, on a subject that was preoccupying him: the
reclamation of the Sahara Desert.

It was not such a fantasy as it might seem, and Charles
was not the first to advocate it. In comparatively recent
times – the fifth century BC – the historian Herodotus
described forests, animals and cultivated lands 'the equal
of any country in the world'. For the Roman natural
historian Pliny, North Africa – particularly Morocco – was
'the granary of Rome'. As an old man, Pliny watched the

exploitation of Morocco and denounced the Romans for ruining the environment to satisfy their desire for luxury and pleasure.

It was an area so full of wildlife that the emperor Augustus was once able to take 3,500 animals from the region to stock three public games spectacles. But the area was gradually stripped of organic matter and deforested on a massive scale to provide fuel for heating the public baths in Rome and timber for the manufacture of furniture and ships.

Without any land management or reforestation at all, the soil, which itself had been over-cropped to provide grain for Rome, was washed away by the rains. There was no fertilising or feeding of the ground, and dustbowls and sand took over; and through the centuries that followed, invasions and conflicts also played their part in reducing a once lush and well-populated area to an empty wilderness, in which can still be seen today from the air the relics and artefacts of vanished cultures and road systems.

Charles's visit to Morocco after Blanche's death had rekindled his interest in the area. In 1963 he had written to Sir Norman Wright, the Secretary for the British Association for the Advancement of Science, suggesting that oil could be processed to provide organic fertiliser as a way of combating world hunger. Surface excavations in the desert often revealed rich soil below the sun-baked surface sand; the water resources beneath the Sahara had sometimes been called its 'subterranean lake'. Moreover, growth was abundant around oases, which were the points at which subterranean water came to the surface. Were one to attempt to reclaim the water that undoubtedly lay beneath the Sahara, and use it to revive the arid desert, there was abundant oil to fuel the machinery, and oil itself, being organic in origin, could be converted into natural fertilisers and play a vital part in nourishing the crops.

Sir Norman had replied that this was not technically

possible, but Charles remained unconvinced. Now, three years later, he knew that Esso Petroleum had indicated that there *were* possibilities of using oil in just that way.

As Charles had looked in 1966 at the vast expanse of the Sahara, he realised that such a province, reclaimed and productive, could provide food in quantities that would solve the starvation crisis of a hemisphere. And he reflected that the development of the earth's large arid and unproductive areas was as thrilling a challenge as one could imagine. At that time he was reminded of the words of the prophet Isaiah about the restoration of the desert places:

> The desert and parched land will be glad:
>   the wilderness will rejoice and blossom . . . .
> Water will gush forth in the wilderness
>   and streams in the desert.
>
> The burning sand will become a pool,
>   the thirsty ground bubbling springs.
> In the haunts where the jackals once lay,
>   grass and reeds and papyrus will grow.
>
> (Isa. 35:1, 6-7)

So it was that he made contact with H.S. Darling again, as a result of an article he wrote on the subject for the Christian paper *Challenge* in 1975. Its editor, Derek Sangster, sent a copy to Dr Darling, who was a distinguished agriculturalist and therefore in a position to influence opinion on the matter.

Dr Darling's reply was cautious in the extreme, pointing out that nobody really knew how much water was below the Sahara, and that the costs of any irrigation and canalisation project would be prohibitive. He echoed the caution of Sir Norman Wright, and, in view of the lack of well-designed feasability studies, regretfully declined to be involved in Charles's proposals.

There is no doubt that Dr Darling represented the bulk

of academic and professional thinking about the prospects for reclamation, but Charles was not willing to abandon his cause. Over the next twelve months he wrote to numerous influential people in politics and agriculture, including Henry Kissinger (the adviser to the US President), Sir Maurice Laing (Sir John's successor in the family company), Brian Griffiths the political economist, and others. He produced one of his duplicated documents, entitled *Food for All and Work for All*, and distributed it. He encountered some encouragement and a considerable amount of scepticism.

But world opinion was changing, and Charles found a great deal to encourage him. In 1975, an enthusiastic letter came from George W. Target, an author whose controversial views and unorthodox books gave him much in common with Charles. Interest was shown by TEAR Fund, by an Anglican Rural Development organisation, and by a number of firms active in dry areas of the world.

In 1976, the newspapers reported that Dr Kissinger was proposing a programme to combat drought in African dry regions by 'rolling back the desert'. A British-based company, Peabody Galion Corporation, won a £50,000,000 contract to process 900 tons of domestic refuse per day from Tripoli and Benghazi, as part of Libya's plan to reclaim the desert.

In 1977, Egypt announced the discovery of one of the largest underground reservoirs in the world. It was claimed that it extended from the Red Sea mountains down to the border with Libya, and that it contained about 524,000,000 cubic yards of water ready to be tapped for irrigation. In September 1977 the *Harvester* magazine reported that Dr Darling had been appointed to a new post, and in December, *Challenge* ran an article headed 'The Lake Under The Sahara':

Two years ago *Challenge* interviewed C.F. Fraser-Smith who insisted that there was water below parts of the Sahara Desert which could be tapped to make the desert bloom.

But the experts were not impressed.

> Said Dr H.S. Darling, then principal of Wye Agricultural College, 'I am not sanguine about prospects for success of Mr Fraser-Smith's proposals to exploit the waters said to be below the Sahara. In my view the whole idea is a very doubtful starter.'
>
> This year the prospect of using water from lakes 1,000 metres below the Sahara received a final boost from the Egyptian Government who plan to tap part of an underground lake . . ..
>
> The discovery is the result of an 18-month survey by an international team. According to Egypt's semi-official daily *Al Abram*, Britain's Dunlop and the Chase Manhattan Bank are two of the firms concerned with a scheme 'which could revolutionise the economy of the Western Desert'.
>
> Dr H.S. Darling, now Director General of the International Centre for Agricultural Research in Dry Areas (ICARDA), is very interested in research on the underground lake.

One gains the impression that Charles and Derek Sangster relished their vindication!

Of course, it would be an exaggeration to say that Charles was a major force in bringing about a rethinking on the desert economy. But the episode illustrates his characteristic tenacity and tireless enthusiasm for causes in which he passionately believed. The Sahara impinged on several of his most important concerns: his dream of a united Europe – even a united world – working together for the good of all humanity; his deep commitment to the people of North Africa; his desire that missionaries should involve themselves in the practical needs of the people to whom they ministered.

Charles's interest in world agriculture had also been applied much closer at hand. At Aylescott Farm, a major shift of policy had been introduced; in 1967 Brian had decided that the farm was unlikely to remain viable as a dairy unit, and had taken the major step of restructuring the entire operation as a crop drying plant. This meant that the whole of the pasture was grown to cut five times a year, and a grass drier and compressing plant were installed. The farm produce was now high-protein-value dried grass pellets, and specialised cattle feeds, including dried grass.

It was a logical step forward. Charles's first innovations had been in his approach to pasture, and the fields at Aylescott were famous for their rich food content and efficient management. He had built up the farm into a high-yield unit, and had become widely known for his often controversial writings on such subjects as autumn pasture values and high quality silage. Now those resources of pasture had been used to form the basis of the new plant.

Not for the first time, Charles and now Brian found themselves swimming against the tide of popular opinion. Grass, harvested, dried and compressed into pellets and cubes had been pioneered in the 1940s in Britain. Charles's wartime broadcasts to North Africa had pioneered the cubing of dehydrated potatoes and other foods for the forces. But in the 1950s and early 1960s grass-drying had declined because imported foodstuff for cattle was much cheaper.

During the 1970s protein cattle-feed imports to the UK and EEC countries became expensive. Decisions were taken to ensure that home-produced sources of proteins were safeguarded by a support system. High-protein crops of dried grass (and lucerne grown in France) were therefore essential. A fluctuating subsidy to ensure a viable industry was started – high market prices, low support; low prices, higher support.

As a result the European production has grown to two

million tonnes of high-protein home-produced cattle feed, saving the Community several hundred million pounds of revenue on imports. This helped the late 1980s cereal problem by taking acreage out of cereal production. Efficient grass drying not only produced the highest protein output per acre of any alternative crop, but also yielded high levels of energy. This protein and energy is a 'natural' feed with no additives, and is very valuable for the ruminant animal.

In the late 1960s, from his knowledge of animal nutrition acquired from Charles and the dairy herd management, Brian believed that the philosophy of natural feed would become increasingly important. During the 1970s and 1980s Brian became involved with, and held office in, British and European trade and research organisations and EEC commissions. His belief in the value of simply grown, naturally produced grass as a valuable asset for cattle feeding was vindicated.

After many years of producing dried feed for cattle, Brian is now involved with experimental production of proteins for humans from fresh grass. He is thus completing the cycle which began with Charles's involvement with dried food for humans in the 1940s.

The experimental system uses only mechanical energy and steam to produce a very high protein curd, which is edible for humans. Though the process was discovered in the 1930s, it is still regarded as a bizarre and non-viable idea. However, responding to work being done to aid countries with low-protein diets, Brian is now looking seriously at the long-term possibilities, not only in 'Third World' countries but particularly in Europe.

Brian's proposals therefore offer a natural product, produced naturally to enrich the human diet. And they originate in Charles's initial interest in, and firmly-held views on, the value of grass grown in a proper manner.

It is a characteristic illustration of the way Charles's mind worked. The great dream was the Sahara, its massive

resources of water and potential fertility waiting only for
international co-operation and goodwill for systematic
reclamation to begin. But while the world waited for that
miracle to happen, individuals could make a difference:
as at the family farm at Aylescott, where grass-drying
provided a tantalising glimpse of a technology that offered
boundless potential to a hungry world – cheap protein,
food that would not deteriorate in store; even, it was
claimed, protein produced direct from grass without the
intervention of a cow at all.

Charles says:

> We have still to face an ever-increasing and hungry
> world population as, according to *World Resources
> 1988-89*, the population of the world grew by
> 84,000,000 in 1988 and is likely to reach six billion by
> 1998. We have the knowledge and the technique to
> meet this demand for food – the American Ministry of
> Agriculture, after analysing grass output at Aylescott
> twenty-five years ago, reported it as the best in protein
> value with the maximum production, and stated that
> farmers world-wide had hardly started exploiting this
> superb potential.

In 1963, he wrote in *Crusade* magazine that grass
husbandry is the oldest subject in the world, and the most
neglected. After the creation of dry land, the first
recorded thing created is grass; and the Old Testament
repeatedly refers to its potential and its need for wise
management. All essential foods come from grass, such
as milk, butter, cheese, meat and grain. And it builds up
superb humus in the soil.

It is interesting too, he pointed out, that grass drying is
mentioned in two of the Gospels: '. . . the grass of the
field, which is here today and tomorrow is cast into the
oven' (Matt. 6:30, Luke 12:28, AV).[29] In his travels in
Scotland he discovered that a century ago the Scots dried
their grass in large ovens; and the mention in the book of

Daniel that Nebuchadnezzar 'ate grass like cattle' for seven years (Dan. 5:21) prompted him to speculate what the full nutritional value of grass might be, were it to be systematically and efficiently exploited.

One of the great disappointments in Charles's life was the rejection of his proposition, put to the Foreign Office, that in areas subject to disaster there should be set up stores of tightly-compressed food cubes similar to grass cubes. They would have many economic advantages, be easily distributed, and would only need the addition of water to make them edible (if not too palatable); it would be an effective emergency measure to combat immediate need. The idea was received with considerable enthusiasm, but nothing at all was heard further from the government.

CHAPTER FIFTEEN
The Word of Life

Charles's interest in the problems of a hungry world was not merely political or economic. He saw little point in filling people's stomachs if no attempt were to be made to feed their hearts as well. It was an urgent and biblical necessity to find food for those who were physically starving. But if that was as far as aid went, all that was happening was that a temporary remedy had been provided.

'The mind and body cannot be separated,' he said repeatedly. 'It is the Bible alone that can help people to evaluate themselves and the world in which they live.'

He was not simply uttering evangelical slogans. For Charles, the Bible is a totality; it contains God's entire way of salvation for humanity, but it also provides the best guidance on daily life, relationships, wisdom, law and understanding.

Hence his commitment to the work of the Bible Society, an organisation that furthers knowledge and distribution of the Scriptures all over the world, and has an unusually high level of awareness of current affairs, modern media, and contemporary social structures. Charles joined the Barnstaple and District Branch with Blanche when they moved to Barnstaple, and his links continued through the years. He was elected Chairman of the Branch, and tackled the job with the enthusiasm and lack of respect for convention which he brought to most enterprises. His view of the work of the Bible Society is summed up in a newsletter he produced as Chairman in the 1970s:

I think the Bible Society is not just a good cause. It is the essential work of the Church. Whilst it is necessary for the Church to be moved with compassion for the homeless and for the hungry people of the world, we should be failing in our job as a Christian community if we did not provide for them the very thing it is our task to provide, that is, the spiritual food of the Scriptures. So when you are working on behalf of the Bible Society you are really doing one of the essential tasks of the Church – distributing the Word of God.

During the 1970s, the project that dominated the activities of the Barnstaple and District Branch was that of raising funds for a new Arabic Bible.

There was already, of course, a modern Arabic Bible in existence. Captain Fisk had concentrated all his energies on producing it before Moroccan Independence and the certain expulsion of the missionaries. His great work had been completed in 1957. But a devastating blow awaited him. The British and Foreign Bible Society had to decline to publish the translation, because the work's area of usefulness was limited to Morocco. Much as they desired to make Fisk's labours available in printed form, the money simply did not exist with which to publish for such a small market.

It is difficult to imagine the effect that such a decision must have had on a man who was no longer young and had devoted several years and a great deal of prodigious effort to the task. But it was a measure of the stature of the man that he accepted the decision as just. He returned to his labours.

Three years later, after immense effort, he had completed a new translation that was suitable for the entire 2,000 mile stretch of North Africa. He brought the manuscript to London, together with a cheque for £3,000 representing money sent to him by various friends, and called on Sir John Laing. Laing contributed a similar amount of money, and together they went to Bible House, the headquarters of the Bible Society. The Society agreed to sponsor publication, at a total cost of £10,000.

Eric Fisk's work had resulted in a Bible which had been of enormous value. At a Press conference, Charles had listened to Arabs from several different North African countries read from it fluently. Much later he visited Sir John Laing, then in his nineties, and was able to tell him that the word of God was being spread throughout North Africa, and to give him news of an elderly colleague of Captain Fisk still living in Morocco. Charles visited Sir John shortly before he died, and he showed Charles with deep satisfaction a specially bound copy of Fisk's Arabic Bible which the Bible Society had presented to him.

Much of Charles and Blanche's involvement with the Bible Society had been to raise funds for the publication of that translation.

In 1969 Captain Fisk died. Charles felt his loss deeply. 'He was a true man of God,' he recalled in later years. 'I found him a great disciplinarian, but he was warm-hearted and free from anything ostentatious. There was a certain greatness in the man – a Godly greatness.' He died a life governor of the Bible Society (an honour which was also to be bestowed upon Charles).

Charles wrote an obituary for the Christian Brethren Research Fellowship's newsletter. He suggested that a Fisk Memorial Fund should be set up, that an appropriate way of acknowledging his memory would be to continue his work. And the best way of doing that, he proposed, was by producing an up-to-date Arabic translation which would speak to a new generation of Islam.

For Islam was changing, and the rate of change had accelerated beyond any expectations. In the new climate of education and modernity in the Muslim world, and with a language that was changing, Captain Fisk's work was beginning to show its limitations.

Charles's proposal was for a new translation, written in the kind of Arabic that was used in Arabic daily newspapers, so that readability and interesting writing would attract readers. He emphasised the need to use journalists rather than pure Arabic stylists in the translation.

Eventually the Bible Society agreed to produce a 'TAV' – 'Today's Arabic Version'. The cost, which would have to be met by fundraising and gifts, would be £87,000.

Charles began his own local fundraising attempts by showing stereoscopic slides of Morocco, taken by a Frenchman in the first years of the twentieth century. They were informative, interesting, and hardly anybody came to see them.

He went back to the beginning and rethought his strategy. There was a growing interest and concern in conservation and care for the environment. Charles had an idea. He spent the next few weeks with his camera exploring the coombes, hills and rivers of Exmoor and the North Devon coastline. Soon posters were appearing locally.

**BRITAIN'S GREATNESS IN NATURE
– BRITAIN'S GREATEST NEED**
Colourful Slides of North Devon
40 miles of magnificent coastline
(with some of its 40 coastal waterfalls)

The meetings were a departure from the usual local church meetings, and many people came who would not normally have attended a Christian event, and they heard the gospel there. The proceeds of the meetings went towards the new Bible, and with attendances of 250 or more, a very satisfactory amount was raised.

Charles and his committee members also organised visits by public speakers who had links with Morocco: Albert Fallaize, Charles Marsh, the author of a number of Christian books, and Professor F.F. Bruce were among those who drew interested audiences. There were several more besides, drawn from different church traditions.

As the years went by, many North Devon churches

became very committed to supporting the work of the Bible Society, and under Charles's chairmanship regular and substantial contributions were made.

But the fundraising and the steadily growing Fisk Memorial Fund were not only local activities. One morning a letter from the Faeroe Islands, in the North Atlantic, arrived for Charles. A cheque made out to the Fisk Memorial Fund was enclosed, and a short note which read:

> We forward a cheque trusting it is the guidance of the Spirit of God to make us support this work. May God bless His Word. Isa. 55.10-13.

The obituary which Charles had written had been translated and reprinted in a Danish periodical. Elizabeth Joanesarson, a policeman's wife, had read it, and it was she who had sent the cheque.

From that first letter a correspondence developed between Charles and the Faeroese Christians, which culminated in a three-week visit in 1973 in which Charles met Christians, many of them members of Open Brethren churches, in the various islands. He was immensely impressed by the quality of Faeroese society, its extraordinarily low crime levels and the unusually large numbers of professing Christians; and he was moved and astonished by the support which they gave to the Fisk Memorial Fund and to Christian work in general. A series of articles which he wrote in the *Harvester* on his return spoke warmly of the character of the 40,000 people in the Islands, and recalled the bravery and steadfastness of the Islanders during the war.

Through Elizabeth Joanesarson the Faeroese sent a total of £2,300 to the fund, and Barnstaple and District Bible Society raised £2,400.

When the new translation was published, half a million copies were sold in twelve months. A copy was presented to Anwar Sadat, the President of Egypt, and he took it with him on his historic peace initiative to Israel in 1977, where he read from it at the Israeli Parliament, the Knesset. Some who heard the reading were very appreciative of the translation.

Charles's work for the Bible Society did not mean that he forgot his other interests. He was still passionately concerned about world hunger and the work of the United Nations and the Save the Children Fund.

In October 1977, he had the opportunity to attend, as an observer, the deliberations of the thirty-second General Assembly of the United Nations in New York. He listened fascinated to debates on the Arab-Israeli conflict, on Cyprus, and on South Africa and Rhodesia. In the Economic and Social Council Hall he heard how over 800 million children were being helped through UNESCO and UNICEF, and absorbed with some awe the statistic that smallpox had declined from an average 21 million cases per annum to approximately 400 cases.

He was impressed by the technical wizardry of the building (simultaneous translations of the debates in several languages were available on headphones), and also by the efficient security measures. He listened to one debate with three agricultural students from different parts of the world. One of the students surreptitiously took out a pocket camera and took a discreet photograph. An electronic sensing device picked up the noise of the shutter, and within seconds a policeman had arrived and courteously but firmly ejected the photographer.

The processes of the Council greatly impressed him. He responded to the spectacle of the cut and thrust of debate, where not long before nations had attacked each other with guns. He sensed that the great words carved at the entrance to the United Nations were being fulfilled:

They shall beat their swords into ploughshares, and their spears into pruning hooks, nation shall not lift up sword against nation, neither shall they learn war any more. (Isa. 2:4)

He had not lost his eye for agricultural detail, and noted that in the grounds of the building were planted 2,000 rose bushes, 185 flowering cherry trees, and a wide variety of shrubs and flowers donated by various countries. And over all, to summarise the UN manifesto and Charles's hopes for a saner world, the flags of the nations fluttered endlessly in line.

Back in Barnstaple, Charles wrote to his local newspaper:

It was heart-warming and brought a surge of hope for our somewhat disunited world . . .. Let us co-operate socially, politically, and be united and strong to withstand any other world power who may want to dominate us militarily, politically, or commercially.

Yet he knew that though he believed he had seen people of good will genuinely striving for a more united, compassionate and just world, it remained a human institution. Man's security and future did not lie in the councils of politicians, but in God's Son, Jesus Christ, as presented in the word of God, the Bible.

So he continued in his efforts to distribute the word of God in whatever way possible.

The media were very interested, for example, when in 1978 he discovered a version of the Gospel of Matthew in West Devon dialect in the library of the British and Foreign Bible Society. He obtained permission to reprint a facsimile of some of the pages together with notes on pronunciation, and the leaflet that resulted sold several thousand copies. Orders were received from all over Britain, and from abroad. The Press, radio and television all ran features, and the local M.P., Jeremy Thorpe, took a personal interest in the leaflet.

The history of the version that Charles had discovered goes back to Napoleon, whose nephew commissioned the translation. In *Four Thousand Year War*, Charles put forward the possibility that the document had some connection with nineteenth-century Dartmoor Prison, where French prisoners are known to have been held.[30] The printing of the leaflet was underwritten by the Bible Society, and the proceeds were donated to the Society.

Living, as he did, on the edge of Exmoor, Charles noticed that more and more farms were offering bed-and-breakfast, and that the tourist industry was opening up all over Devon. It was an area he loved, and he knew it well, having walked over most of it.

Holding such a deep concern for the distribution of the word of God, it was inevitable that Charles should have come into contact with the Gideons, an international group famous for their work of placing Bibles in hotel rooms. Charles contacted Gideons headquarters and made a suggestion. Why not extend the work to placing Bibles in bedrooms in bed-and-breakfast houses?

It took considerable correspondence between Charles, the Gideons, the National Trust, and other interested bodies, but eventually Charles was given the go-ahead. Between 1977 and 1981, he personally placed 350 Bibles in farm houses and hotels all over Exmoor, on behalf of the Gideons International.

There was much good will. One farmer's wife, Mrs Pat Symons, accepted a Gideon Bible and asked, 'Is this the same as the Bible that is placed in the lockers at Barnstaple Hospital? I am on night duty there twice a week. I had a very depressed patient and I read to him from the Gideon Bible for almost an hour. It was wonderful to see him completely reassured.'

He was always alert for any opportunity, either to distribute the word of God himself or to raise money for the work of the Bible organisations. When his home village of Bratton Fleming was twinned with a French village in Normandy, Charles was invited to write a short historical brochure. In the end, the Twinning committee decided that they could not afford to put the project into print. Charles decided to print it himself and give the proceeds to the Gideons. It was published in 1980, and a good number were sold in Normandy and in Devon. One purchaser sent Charles a £10 note without giving her address, because, she said, she knew how much printing cost and felt guilty at being asked to pay only twenty pence for the brochure.

In his Bible distribution work, Charles met only three refusals. One guest house was run by Mormons, who declined on the grounds that 'We have our own Bible'; a farmer refused, claiming to be an atheist; and a riding centre said no. 'Our clients would rather have a bottle of whisky by their beds than a Bible.'

Charles never lost sight of the fact that for the Christian, life is a war situation. Although he enjoyed his work for the Gideons, and met almost universal friendliness and appreciation, he was under no illusion that the matter was anything but desperately urgent. In the summer of 1980 he sent to various Gideon officials a cutting from the Cairo *Evening News* dated 12 March 1980:

The Ministry of Religion is in the process of printing 50,000 of an English translation of the Glorious Qur'an for the world. The translator is Abdullah Yussef El-Hindi. The Ministry is undertaking with the hotel companies in Egypt to put a copy of the Qur'an in every room of the biggest tourist hotels and to distribute some of the copies to our overseas embassies and Islamic and Culture centres with the aim of encouraging religious tourism and to increase the numbers of tourists from Islamic countries.

But there were great encouragements. When the Hilton Hotel at Gatwick Airport was opened (one of the architects of which was Charles's son-in-law), the Gideons placed 333 Bibles in the bedrooms. Later the General Manager wrote a gracious note of thanks to the Gideons concerned:

> The simple ceremony and dedication made us all recognise the tremendous value of the Gideon Bible, and we appreciated this peaceful interlude during the final hours before the opening.
> I hope that you will have the opportunity to visit us frequently, and trust that you will look on us as Friends of the Gideons. Please do not hesitate to contact me if we can ever be of any assistance to the Society.

It was a similar story in Trust House Forte, when Sir Charles Forte, the owner of over 800 hotels, was presented with the ten millionth copy of the Gideon Bible distributed in Britain.

Throughout Britain, the work proceeds methodically. In the schools, for example, a New Testament is presented to every child during their first year at a senior school.

It was, and remains, a quiet ministry, which receives little publicity. Its members go about their work quietly, and the large number of stories of people whose lives have been touched and often transformed by finding a Gideon Bible within reach at a crucial time do not often find their way into the sensational Press.

Yet in 1981, the media had a good deal to say about Charles's work with Gideons International. In fact, they had a good deal to say about every aspect of Charles's life. For Charles had become a person of absorbing interest to many people. His first book, *The Secret War of Charles Fraser-Smith*, had been published; and everybody wanted to interview him.

CHAPTER SIXTEEN

Charles Fraser-Smith, Author

At school, Charles had been poor at English, and he never passed an examination in the subject. The shadow of the First World War dominated his schooldays. The best of the young English teachers had been called up, and Charles was taught by retired elderly schoolmasters who had been invited back to fill the gaps. As a result, Charles and many of his classmates were able to avoid hard work in an uncongenial subject and were without the spark of encouragement that only a gifted and enthusiastic teacher can provide. As he later described it laconically, 'We got away with it.'

As an adult he was a competent linguist and a good manager, and he never had any need to repair the gap in his education. The articles he wrote were mainly factual, full of stark (and provocative) assertions and efficiently-marshalled facts and figures. His letters and the duplicated documents he produced for the local Bible Society and other causes he championed were like his speech – enthusiastic, pulling out an enormous range of references from the Bible and from his own multitude of experiences, full of the passion of one who knows that many of his readers will probably disagree with him. But polished, finished literary pieces they were not.

Not everybody was convinced that writing articles was an effective use of time. A Christian friend one day remarked to Charles,

'Writing those articles must take a lot of time . . . and

you don't make much money out of it, do you? Is it worth it? Or is it just a waste of time?'

Charles knew what that meant; a 'better' use of time would be attending Christian conferences, or perhaps preaching. He was sure he would be no good at the latter, and the former was hardly an option for somebody who had returned from Morocco and begun farming in Britain at the age of 47, with a heavy mortgage and family responsibilities. He was sixty at the time of the conversation, an age when people tend to have more leisure; but his financial obligations and his restless energy left little time for the literary life beyond the matter-of-fact, technical information contained in his farming articles.

Yet the conversation with his friend lingered in his mind. Why not use his agricultural experience and his recollections of life in Morocco as the basis for articles which would be a commentary on various subjects, all from the perspective of a biblical view of farming?

So articles appeared from Charles's pen in a number of Christian magazines and newspapers, all arising from his agricultural activities and his Christian faith. For example, a 1963 article in *Crusade* began:

> The author of this article is well known in agricultural circles in Britain for his revolutionary ideas about grass. Leading farming journals have investigated his claims to raise the standards of his herds by raising the quality of the grass in his pastures. What they do not say, however, is that Mr. Fraser-Smith – for many years a missionary in North Africa – arrived at these views because he believes man has a stewardship of the soil committed to him by God; and it is man's duty to see that the soil is wisely and productively used.[31]

The *Harvester*, *Challenge* and several other publications printed contributions from Charles, and he began to have as considerable a reputation among Christian readers as he had among the agricultural community. Thus, for most of his adult life, Charles wrote prolifically.

However, for many years he had no thought of publishing what he wrote as a book. The first time he seriously considered such an idea was in the autumn of 1977, when he was visiting his daughter in New York, on the visit already referred to in connection with the United Nations.

Christine's husband, Alan Williams, was an architect with Hiltons International. At the time he was writing a book on toys. 'You should write one too,' he said to Charles. 'On toys. Your wartime toys – the secret gadgets.'

'That's preposterous,' Charles replied. 'I've no idea how to write a book. Anyway, I've no time. And who would want to publish it?'

But Alan pressed the matter enthusiastically. 'You wouldn't have to do the writing. Just tell the story. Half the books you see in the shops are ghost-written. You just tell the story to a writer and they write it down and make a book out of it. Yours is a story that ought to be told.'

In the weeks and months that followed, Charles was unable to forget Alan's suggestion. He was right; providing the right ghost-writer could be found, writing a book would be a simple matter. And there was a story there to be told. Charles had kept a collection of his wartime gadgets, and so far as he knew he was the only person alive who possessed such a collection or had such a detailed knowledge of the role they had played and the people and firms who had made them. And the biggest obstacle had already been overcome: the Official Secrets Act, which Charles had signed so long ago, had bound him to absolute secrecy over his war work for thirty years. But now the period of silence was past, and he was free to speak.

He began to make enquiries, to find out who were the publishers likely to be interested in such a book. Eventually the proposal landed on the desk of Alan

Brooke, the Managing Director of Michael Joseph, a London publisher. He visited Charles in Barnstaple, and shortly afterwards Gerald McKnight, the ghost writer, came to Barnstaple.

Two ghost writers worked on the book, which was published in 1981 under the title *The Secret War of Charles Fraser-Smith: the 'Q' Gadget Wizard of World War II*. Charles was somewhat disappointed that the finished book contained relatively few of his outspoken Christian statements. But enough of his highly individual views, and his remarkable life, characterises the book for the reader to understand that this is no conventional story of espionage and undercover work.

The book aroused a great deal of interest, and Dale Cottage in Bratton Fleming was suddenly busy and full of strangers with microphones and cameras.

On Sunday 20 December 1981, Secret War was featured on the 'Sixty Minutes' programme of CBS News. It followed Nancy Reagan's Christmas broadcast, and Charles sent her a copy of the book, receiving a pleasant acknowledgement.

In Britain, Television South-West made a half-hour documentary which won a television award, and also featured Charles in two religious programmes. He appeared in the children's programme 'Freeze Frame', and in several other programmes.

Interest in the book continued, and Charles received many letters from overseas, including correspondence from people who had used, or whose parents had used, the gadgets described in the book. One fascinating acquaintance gained this way was with the American, Keith Melton, who was in USA Naval Intelligence, a concessionaire of a chain of fast-food restaurants in Louisiana, and the owner of a house which was a replica of an English castle. For over eighteen years, Keith Melton had been collecting secret equipment from the wartime secret departments, and had managed to obtain specimens of many of Charles's gadgets. His collection of secret equipment numbered over 1,000 items, and he has now written a book on *Clandestine Warfare: Weapons and Equipment of the SOE and OSS* (Blandford Press). Another book under preparation is *MIS-X: Secret Aid to POWs*, by Lloyd R Shoemaker. MIS-X is the American equivalent of the British MI9. Both books pay warm tribute to Charles's work and achievements in his unique position in World War II. Writing to Charles, Lloyd Shoemaker remarked, 'Your name and work are often mentioned to the Senior Class at the US Air Force Academy.'

The letters 'MIS-X' were Charles's idea. MIS was his own code for the supply of secret gadgets to British POWs, and he added the letter X to indicate American prisoners of war. On America's entry into the war, Lloyd Shoemaker with three colleagues came to London to study methods of escape and evasion, and to see how British expertise could be applied to USA Service.

A paperback edition of *Secret War* appeared in 1983, and by 1984 sales had justified a second printing, followed by a large third impression in 1986.

In 1983, Charles and Lin travelled to Plymouth to appear on Television South-West with Desmond Llewelyn, the actor who plays 'Q' in the James Bond films. The occasion was the forthcoming charity gala performance of the Bond film 'Octopussy'. The close resemblance of the two men took everybody by surprise; they looked like brothers.

After a brief rehearsal and lunch, Charles was shown the gadgets that had been used in the film. They were fascinating: a gold Mont Blanc fountain pen, valued at £700, modified to shoot acid; a Faberge egg that – even though an imitation – must have cost hundreds of pounds to make, its interior lovingly packed with a tiny coach and horses and an even smaller microphone; a wristwatch television, using liquid crystal electronics that are commercially available today.

In the interview that followed, Charles showed some of his own gadgets and talked about the job that he had done during the war. But he acknowledged that James Bond had access to much superior technology: 'My gadgets are old rope, compared to James Bond's!'

Charles's gadgets found a permanent home in Bickleigh Castle, near Tiverton in Devon. They have been exhibited there each summer since 1983, and Charles and Lin frequently spend 'signing' days at the castle, autographing copies of his books. The gadgets on display, some sixty items, represent only a fraction of the equipment that Charles was responsible for; yet it is one of the most comprehensive collections of such devices in existence.

At signing days, the reactions of the various visitors are striking. Visitors from Germany, for example, are greatly intrigued by the exhibits. French and Dutch visitors often express deep and moving gratitude to Britain for her part in the war. And many who visit the castle, whose fathers have at home a treasured memento of the war – a button compass, a silk map or some other gadget – are delighted to find, in *Secret War*, a unique book that sets them in the context in which they were used.

When the gadgets went on display for the season in 1984, there were two books to be sold alongside them. *Secret Warriors: Hidden Heroes of MI6, OSS, MI9, SOE & SAS* was the result of a correspondence that began when Charles wrote to a journalist, Kevin Logan, congratulating him for his firm and courageous writing. They began a correspondence that continued.

Kevin Logan later became an Anglican clergyman. He was Curate-in-Charge of St John's Church, Leyland, when Charles mentioned that he had been working on a manuscript about the people who had used his gadgets in the war. He offered Logan the job of ghost-writing the book, and the invitation was accepted. He began the project during a stay in hospital.

Charles's reasons for writing the book are summed up

in his Preface, where he describes the books that his son-
in-law Alan made him read in preparation for *Secret War*
in 1977:

> My assault on this mountain of military literature
> brought me first to the 'Big Guns' – the statesmen and
> generals, all thundering out their own exploits. Next
> came the historians . . ..
>
> But where were the annals of the real heroes; the
> silent legion whose dangerously-obtained intelligence
> had provided their superiors with their spectacular
> success? . . . May this book help us to appreciate more
> fully the debt which we owe to the small man. In rank,
> he may be small. In retrospect, he is a giant.

It was in 1984, also, that the author of the present book
first became aware of Charles Fraser-Smith, being
commissioned by his publishers Paternoster Press to carry
out the final copy-editing and preparation of the
manuscript for the printer.

There was renewed interest when the book was
published, and one or two newspapers were pleased with
the intriguing matter of the ghost writer's profession.
'Vicar Joins The 007 Brigade!', exclaimed the *Lancashire
Evening Telegraph*. The reviewers were as complimentary
as they had been with the earlier book, and letters came
from young and old. A man who had been a prisoner of
war commented: 'I think your method of whetting the
appetite of your readers for the spiritual message most
ingenious.'

Over the next two years, Charles began to put together a
third book.

Some reviewers had commented that there was a
considerable amount of Christian comment in *Secret
Warriors*; the final chapter was an explicit confession of
faith and appeal to the reader to agree that the only future
for the world lay in Christ.

But the third book, *Men of Faith in the Second World War*, was a straightforwardly Christian assessment of several prominent (and one or two little-known) wartime figures. The individuals chosen ranged from Field-Marshal Viscount Montgomery to 'Colonel Remy', the brilliant secret agent to whom Charles had sent regular supplies of dominoes. Playing dominoes was a form of password among the French Resistance agents under Remy.

'During the war,' said Charles, 'I had insight into the faith of certain key men – and also, this was a subject that had not been touched on before. The objective was to try to put across the faith and dedication of important men – something which can inspire and encourage us all, young and old.'

Men of Faith was published in 1986, and once again the present author was involved in editing it. The enthusiastic reviews came from magazines as different as the *Preparatory Schools Review* and *Evangelicals Now*. But the most encouraging response was the correspondence that followed its publication. Some of the letters came from readers who had enjoyed the book and found it helpful. One said, 'Your books are the only books my father will read written by a Christian . . .'

Other letters came from relatives of the people whom Charles had written about in the book. A daughter of Air Chief Marshal Sir Wilfrid Freeman wrote:

I was recently given a copy of your book *Men of Faith* and was amazed and delighted to find that it contained an account of my father's work. Amazed, because the loss of his personal papers has made him a difficult subject for any author; and delighted, because you have described him and his work so well that I have ordered copies for all my children.

An appreciative letter came from the grandson of Field-Marshal Viscount Montgomery, who had previously

visited the Fraser-Smiths for an evening meal, and a
member of the family of General Sir Arthur Smith wrote
to say that the book had meant a great deal to Sir Arthur's
widow.

There were many similar letters. Charles valued them not
only because they were appreciative of his work, but also
because they added to his knowledge of the men he had
written about. It was a book written out of great
admiration, and any additional item of information was a
source of real satisfaction to Charles. (There were
sometimes discoveries to be made, too: we have already
seen in chapter seven how such a correspondence solved
the mystery of the real identity of Colonel Dansey,
Charles's superior in MI6.[32])

In 1987, Peter Cousins, Editorial Director of Paternoster
Press, composed a Press release for the publication of
Charles's fourth book.

> Few men become authors in their seventies. But
> Charles Fraser Smith has written no fewer than three
> best-selling books about World War Two since his
> seventy-fourth birthday . . .

The new book was something of a departure for Charles.
It was an ambitious survey of life as lived in a world
dominated by an eternal and invisible conflict; that
between good and evil. Though it opens with military
stories and discussions of strategic successes of past wars,
the book devotes most of its 160 pages to a consideration
of topics such as Armageddon, world hunger, ecology,
and similar subjects. There is a chapter about the Sahara,
in which he summarises his challenge to reclamation, and
an extended discussion of whole food and growing one's
own vegetables.

Entitled *Four Thousand Year War*, it is as close as
Charles has yet come to a specifically evangelistic book,

and the challenge it presents to the reader is very clear.

Charles wrote it at full speed in his habitual long-hand, the same neat, evenly sloping characters that fills the notebook of suppliers which is his only tangible souvenir today of his wartime office in MI6. It was a huge book by the time he had finished, and he decided that he needed a ghost writer to reduce it in size to a normal pocket paperback. Paternoster Press suggested the writer of the present book, and so Four Thousand Year War appeared over the names 'Charles Fraser-Smith with David Porter'.

To bring the story of Charles's books up to date, the history of the present book is that it was conceived at the end of 1987, and I began work on it the following January. Charles has provided his usual sheaves of hand-written notes, and I have independently researched many of the areas covered. Charles has scrutinised each section of the book as it has been completed, and suggestions have also been provided by Peter Cousins of Paternoster Press.

This biography is therefore a unique mix of ghost biography, biography, and extended treatise on a number of subjects. The opinions expressed in the book about issues and controversies are usually those of Charles; opinions expressed about Charles are always mine. It seems appropriate that Charles, who has never had very much time for the accepted way of doing things, should have a biography that does not fit easily into the normal categories!

Charles's books have introduced him to some unexpected new audiences. His files contain handbills from the National Trust:

> In the Great Hall, with a log fire, three TV films of Charles Fraser-Smith's war work will be shown throughout the day, and the secret gadgets will be on display.

A brochure from the Imperial Hotel, Barnstaple, advertises among the attractions for Christmas at the hotel the following:

> During the afternoon we will have the pleasure of introducing Charles Fraser-Smith, the expert on 'spy gadgetry' during the last war at MI6 and MI9. He will give a talk on his war time experiences. Afternoon tea of muffins and toasted tea cake will round off the talk.

His books have brought invitations to speak at army Christian organisations, churches, and many schools, where he has his own army of young admirers. Fame has brought many interesting people into his life, such as television personality Anneka Rice who sent him a pleasant letter in response to his suggestion that she ought to try out gliding over Exmoor from Devon Airsports, an airfield which Brian had started on the farm.[33]

You might have thought that it would be a wonderful crown to any man's life. After a lifetime of hard work and comparative obscurity, Charles had become a minor celebrity. It was the kind of success to which most people would like to look forward.

But Charles did not see it that way at all. He did not really enjoy the publicity. He was grateful for the opportunity to honour, in his books, some people whose war service had previously been overlooked. But when he looked back on his long and active life, there were other things that he regarded as more important. And when he assessed what might be considered the crowning points of his life, he chose other things than his books.

CHAPTER SEVENTEEN
Handing on the Task

Charles Fraser-Smith was always able to set his hand to several jobs simultaneously, and throughout his life he had been a man who could dream more than one dream. But in the 1980s, though – as we have seen – he had a variety of projects and enterprises to occupy him, one vision above all dominated his life: raising support for Christian work in Arab countries.

It was never something he regarded as a mere second best, 'something he could do' to support a work to which ill health and postwar circumstances had prevented him returning. For Charles, support was a vital part of the missionary enterprise, and he approached the matter with his usual methodical and analytical attitude. 'I have seen so much missionary work hampered,' he wrote in 1988, 'just ticking over – no development, even stagnating, because there is no efficient support system, back-up or fund-raising.'

His approach was the same as it had been to farming, when he had first arrived at Aylescott. Just as he realised that a farm that was not business-minded and efficient had no chance of survival in the tough post-war competitive world, so he had no time for romantic notions of missionary work as funded by a constant stream of miracles, with the church required to do nothing but sit back and admire the handiwork of God.

In Charles's view, the church is a partner with its missionaries in the task of mission, and the church's role

is to provide the financial and other support that is
needed. It is a role that needs to be discharged efficiently,
he argued.

> Unless the work is advertised competently and
> efficiently, how can people give intelligently and will-
> ingly? A restricted approach to finance will mean that
> the work cannot expand.
>
> Yet somehow in many British churches to mention
> money is 'not done'. It is un-British! Generally after a
> missionary meeting people are more interested in
> chatting to their friends than in the collecting box at the
> door.

Such views did not mean that Charles considered
missionary fund-raising to be a human-centred activity.
He placed it firmly in the context of Christian spirituality.
He was fond of quoting the apostle Paul's remarks to the
Corinthian Christians:

> Now about the collection for God's people: Do what I
> told the Galatian churches to do. On the first day of
> every week, each one of you should set aside a sum of
> money in keeping with his income, saving it up, so that
> when I come no collections will have to be made.
> (1 Cor. 16:1–2)

This, Charles pointed out, taught the need for regular,
disciplined and obligatory giving, proportionate to income
and entered into by the whole community of the church.

From his own experience, and that of his close friends,
he knew that missionary work demands the setting of
realistic, achievable targets. But such planning needs a
solid financial base. It is not that the workers on the
mission field should be anything but totally dependent
upon God for their security, financial as well as any other;
it is simply a matter, argued Charles, of the fellowship of

the church, of one part of the body helping and supporting another.

'We may not ourselves be able to go, in obedience to the Master's command,' he once said. 'But at least we can do our utmost to help those who *do* go.'

In his many talks and notes about missionary support, he was adamant that the burden of supporting missionaries must not fall on the shoulders of a few. It is a responsibility of the whole church, and each individual Christian. He described Islam as 'the church's most neglected mission field', and quoted the book of Acts as describing the early church's primary role: to go forth and spread the light, joy and tolerance of the Good News of Jesus Christ, and salvation from the darkness, sadness and intolerance of this world.

'There is no greater enterprise on this earth!' he often explained. 'May we all be partners in this task, by being involved in person, in purse, and in prayer!'

Charles set about the task of challenging the church in North Devon – and further afield – to take up this responsibility. He emphasised that time was short, that missionary giving involved seizing every opportunity.

The Fraser-Smiths' own lives bear witness to that conviction. When conservation was a fashionable word on everybody's lips, and Charles was looking for ways to fund the new Arabic Bible, he organised his slide shows of views of Devon and other places of natural beauty. Lin found that time spent watching television or reading could also be used for knitting; when the present author visited them in 1988, Lin was still making use of every spare moment, working on items which would produce money for TEAR Fund, Arab World Ministries, the Bible Society or one of the other Christian organisations her knitting supports.

The royalties from all Charles's books are donated to Arab World Ministries, and so is the profit from the various ingenious ways that he has devised to promote them: leaflets which describe missionary financial needs and contain order forms for the books are tucked into Charles's letters, and the exhibition of his wartime gadgets at Bickleigh Castle is another source of sales.

In 1985, Charles's sister Edith died. At the remembrance service in Marylebone Parish Church on 28 June, the address was given by Admiral Sir Horace Law, the President of the Officer's Christian Union, where Ede had worked after the war. His address touched on many aspects of the life of an extraordinary woman: her wartime work in Switzerland, helping service men who had escaped from German POW camps; her administrative work in several professional and Christian societies; her involvement with the Billy Graham Crusades, and her deep love of the arts and her quiet ministry to many professional artists and musicians.

Charles had Admiral Law's remarks typed out and duplicated. He sent copies to people who had been unable to attend the funeral, and included an invitation to send donations in memory of Ede Fraser-Smith to either the North Africa Mission or the Officers Christian Union. Including donations made by those attending the funeral, well over a thousand pounds was received by Arab World Ministries, and a further sum was received by the OCU, where it was used to support missionary work done by ex-officers.

It was an entirely appropriate invitation for Charles to offer. It gave Ede's friends the opportunity of a practical act of remembrance that she would have valued more than any other; helping the progress of the missionary work which was so close to her heart.

Any biographer, recording the story of somebody who is still very much alive and whose life has been lived in several countries and encompassed many different activities and more than one career, has a problem of how to finish. As I write these words, at Christmas 1988, Charles and Lin are actively involved in half a dozen projects. Charles's pen is still far from idle; his most recent piece was a letter to the Press in support of Edwina Currie, who resigned her post as Junior Health Minister after her claims of widespread salmonella infection in the egg industry were widely and angrily disputed. Charles took up the cudgels, against the tide, and sent a note of encouragement to Mrs Currie, saying how essential it was that the matter should receive immediate and full investigation.

It's a valuable reminder that neither old age nor retirement mean that a line marked 'finished' can be drawn across anybody's life; Charles has often emphasised, for example, that those who are not missionaries can help support those who are, that those who are prevented from actively helping can still have a crucially important role in praying for missionaries – that nobody, in fact, can claim that they are no longer of use or value.

But it doesn't help the biographer, whose job would be much easier if people's lives stopped being interesting at a certain point after which nothing worth writing about was ever going to happen to them.

Fortunately, Charles himself, towards the end of the 1980s, identified what he saw as the most significant moment for him in the decades since leaving Aylescott. For those who might assume that a successful dairy innovation or a profoundly illuminating overseas trip would be Charles's choice with which to leave the reader, his selection is going to come as something of a surprise.

He singled out an event that happened when he was 80.

To place this in context it is necessary to go back to the early 1970s, when Charles's nephew Keith was training at Clifton Theological College in Bristol.

Keith Fraser-Smith had benefited from the Christian influence of his relatives. His father died when Keith was fourteen, but his mother had brought him up to attend church regularly, and he had two Christian uncles and an

aunt to pray for him regularly. During his secondary
education he became a Christian himself, and also began
to meet Muslim students. At Durham university he began
to pray about missionary work and to develop a concern
for the Muslim world. He was also accepted for training
in the Anglican ministry.

He and his girlfriend spent the summer before
theological college on a work project in Wales. Praying
one morning on a beautiful green hillside, he heard the
voice of God speaking to him clearly.

'You are going to work in the Arab world.'

Keith's reply was spontaneous. 'Lord, you must be
mad! I don't know anyone in the Arab world.'

While he was at Clifton College Charles wrote a letter
to him. He challenged Keith to consider the missionary
implications of Britain's membership of the Common
Market.

. . . I would like to share with you one positive way in
which we can take the initiative in this new situation.
Millions of Muslims from North Africa are coming for
Euro-work. Because we too are in Europe, I see this
influx as the greatest opportunity and the biggest
opening that we have ever had of putting the word of
God into their hands. They can take the Scriptures
back to their own lands which are being closed to the
missionary – perhaps expediently, for God's purposes.
Very often their contracts with European companies
only last a short time, so if you consider the turnover
of personnel you will be staggered by the opportunities
open to us . . ..

Now is the opportunity. Later it could be more difficult as the Islamic Missionary Movement buys redun-
dant churches or builds mosques. Remember that Paul
never stayed put in the face of closed doors – doors
possibly closed by God for His purposes. Rather, he
always moved on seeking open doors . . ..

Keep these things in mind as you consider your call to Muslim work.

Yours,

Uncle Charles.

Keith studied the letter with care; it was later printed in the college's Annual Report.

Keith was ordained, and married Janet Watts, who shared his own call to the Muslim world. The story of their subsequent career is told in Keith's own account, which is included as an appendix to the present book. There he describes how they were led in 1984 to work with the NAM media branch in Marseilles, then called The Radio School of the Bible, with Keith as Director. Three years later, the NAM changed its name to Arab World Ministries, and the media branch became Arab World Media.

Summing up the two causes which had dominated his own life, Charles described them as:

The spreading of the knowledge of the *Bible* through Bible study; and the spreading of the knowledge of the *gospel* through missionary work.

Arab World Ministries is active in both areas. The primary purpose of the centre is Muslim evangelism by means of radio. Bible correspondence courses, literature, and services to the emerging North African Church are also provided. Intensive short-term summer Bible schools have been held in Spain.

The target audience is North African young people between the ages of 18 and 25. A growing number of young people, disillusioned with their social, political and religious environment, are looking for answers to their questions. Foreign radio broadcasts are one of the main focuses of their attention. Radios are widely available and there is freedom of the airwaves.

Recent indications are that every evening there could
be five-figure audiences; over a year, numbers of people
listening at least once could well be in the order of
100,000. The broadcasts are followed up by a comprehensive series of Bible correspondence courses, written or
adapted for the Muslim background, and some other
resources such as an Arabic translation of Navigators
study materials.

Islam has not sat idle under this initiative. A militant
offensive and defensive crusade against Christian broadcasting and influence has been active for some years now
in the Muslim countries. But there is much evidence that
the work of Arab World Ministries is bearing fruit.[34]

Had Charles designed his own Missionary Society to work
in the Arab World, it would have been difficult to fulfil
more closely his ideals for missionary work. Here was an
organisation that had identified the same challenge that
Charles had issued in his letter to Keith at theological
college, in the document he had drafted at the Peabody's
house in Morocco after Blanche died, and on many other
occasions. The doors had closed on the old North Africa
Mission, in the sense that missionaries could work freely
in North Africa. But doors had been flung wide open as
well; and the newly-named Arab World Ministries was
now reaching a new generation of Muslims in a way which
its older incarnation would not have been able to do in
the same way.

Thus, when Charles came to select the moments in his
later life which meant most to him, the one he chose
unhesitatingly as the most important was the appointment
of Keith Fraser-Smith, in 1984, to be Director of Arab
World Media.

It was deeply moving and enormously satisfying for
Charles to see his nephew playing a key role in a work
which so closely identified with his own missionary
priorities.

He often described Keith as carrying on the work in Morocco which he himself had been involved in before the war. He had handed on to a new generation the task to which he had committed most of his adult life: the greatest enterprise on earth.

APPENDIX ONE

Evangelisation of North Africans
(Charles Fraser-Smith)
January 1966

These thoughts which have materialised on returning to Morocco after twenty-five years' absence, however imperfectly expressed, may give a basis for consideration for action.

1. What is the *MAIN OBJECTIVE OF MISSIONARY WORK?*

In the Book of Missionary Activity, i.e. Acts and the Epistles, it is to form churches, and the key-word is mobility, not stability.

The greatest missionary who ever lived never stayed put. If Paul could not form a church – or, when he had formed a church – he did not settle there. He left local persons (N.B. plural) in charge. He did not restrict natural growth and responsibility by his presence. (At times he sent an epistle or a teacher or returned to visit.)

THAT is why these churches grew, even in soil which was as hostile as Morocco.

Have we missionaries thought that our presence and teaching is essential to growth of young churches? And is that one reason why they have not grown and remain inert, or die?

The aim of the first missionaries in Acts/Epistles was to form churches and leave them to develop.

2. What of *MISSIONARY WORK IN NORTH AFRICA?*

There are literally no churches standing on their OWN

feet. The odd few meetings are more or less led by Europeans – westernised in thinking, ways and services.

N.B. While the European is present, the Moroccan will NOT lead. He will always lean and leave it to us. This need of INDIGENOUS CHURCHES is nothing new, of course, but we have got to admit that we or our past methods have not produced local churches. We can produce possibly a dozen excuses and reasons, but . . . .

3. What is the *PRESENT SITUATION OF MISSIONARY WORK IN NORTH AFRICA?*
In North Africa the door is practically closed, but in Europe it is WIDE open (France, Germany, Italy).

a) Arabs go to Europe from *every* village.

b) In Europe they are more approachable – away from tyrannical domination and blind fanaticism. There is freedom of thought and belief. If they believe in Christ and are ALLOWED to develop on Arab lines, they will return to the tens of thousands of villages which missionaries have not touched and will never touch, and influence and win their own people in a way we cannot. If they are persecuted and even killed, which is very doubtful, then 'The blood of the martyr is the seed of the Church'.

c) In Europe God can raise up a North African 'Billy Graham' to start a purely North African movement. Christianity to Arabs is a European product. Christ to Morocco must be a 'Moroccan', not something WE present. They do not want a westernised Christian faith, nor a westernised form of church.

d) There are also opportunities of paramount import-ance in London, Paris, U.S.A. etc. amongst Arab students. These can be welcomed into the home and won. Who can tell what influence they will have as they return to administrative and key positions in their own countries. This is as much missionary work as being actually in a foreign land.

Also, the rising generation should have priority thought. N.B. Fifty per cent of Morocco's population is under 20, and it has one of the fastest growing populations in the world. Many of these 50 per cent will go to Europe, too.

4. What is the *FUTURE OF MISSIONARY WORK AMONGST NORTH AFRICANS?*

Why will not missionaries go where the door is wide open? Paul teaches us to 'shake the dust off our feet'. To retreat to strike elsewhere, or again later. To plough ground that is *not ready* is folly, stubbornness, pride, ignorance and does more harm than good.

One may say: 'If we leave Morocco, we will not be allowed back.' This was not Paul's attitude! Surely we are called to a PEOPLE not just to a place. The Holy Spirit and the Word of God can do their own work (1 Pet. 1:23). Another may say: 'What if we have important work in Morocco?' If churches are being formed, O.K., but e.g., – If a hospital is not forming churches this might need reassessing. – why otherwise pour thousands of pounds annually into it and keep a staff of a dozen, and not fulfil the objective?!

Also, apart from the fact that Europe may be wiser and better for missionary work, it certainly is better for health, education, cheaper living and for proper and essential holidays.

5. *CONCLUSION*

In Morocco there is acute RESTRICTION. This is political *necessity* while a new nation develops, and we do not want to embarrass or jeopardise the future, or Moroccan brethren.

In Europe there is *NO* RESTRICTION. This is the PRESENT potential field for Missionary Work.

WHO is going to seize these opportunities? WHY NOT YOU?

MAY HEARTS BE EXERCISED

Have we faith for this as Paul?

If not, should we not get back home or get right away from the present situation, rut or whatever it is, and re-assess the whole position?

It is only as we go into a 'desert place' and review a situation, that fresh visions and new perspectives are given and balanced thinking re-asserts itself.

So many of us 'rushed' or 'were rushed' into missionary work at too young an age. We had little or no experience or training in business and church life at home, yet we come to the most important occupation in life (missionary work) and to the most difficult of fields (Islamic) without being established in faith, living life, and church work. The question of acquisition of the language at an early age is a false basis, as a man who has kept up Bible study, can always study a language. Remember Christ's 'public service' was three years only of his life, and Paul's 'active service' was short. God gave him a long intellectual schooling and even a training in 'missionary work' against the Christian faith.

Mobile Literary Units

As licences are given for Literature Shops, so one might be obtained for a Mobile Shop, in view of the King's 'Anti-Illiteracy Campaign.'

How advisable it is to have it in Morocco, however, is up to the missionaries to decide. They would definitely want to sell Christian literature as well.

There would be NO difficulty about it in Europe, and it would be no more expensive than renting a house. To keep it going full out, two families would take spells.

It would mean mobility for forming churches.

Literature for Missionary Work (Christian and Secular)

It is according to knowledge gained by reading, that the future of a country is steered towards GOOD or EVIL.

Much of Christian literature is antiquated and unreadable.

We so often have sentimentally boring pet tracts. Too stodgy for words for *non*-Christians.

As the newspaper is the 'bible' of the people, and it is written so that people read it with ease and interest, so should our Christian Literature be written. This is *what* people are used to! In the case of North Africa, the Arabic must not be some pet form we like or are used to, but everyday journalistic language, or as learnt in schools. This is what the majority of the population is learning *now*.

It could be bi-lingual – French/Arabic.

Direct translations with Western mental approach must be avoided!

As 'Church History' is being taught in Moroccan schools, so a missionary edition should be forthcoming – unbiased.

Our foreign imported hymn tunes could not be more unsuitable.

Distribution of Literature

Wise distribution should be studied. NOT given out as litter – or any old how – or barge in on territory where missionaries already are working, without their full consent.

								Charles Fraser-Smith

APPENDIX TWO
Open Doors – Media For Islam
(Keith Fraser-Smith)

It can be difficult to pin-point the first rustlings of the Holy Spirit in a young life. Undoubtedly, having two Christian uncles and an aunt who prayed for me regularly was an essential part of his plan. Twickenham and the rugby internationals provided the excuse to travel with my father to London and the opportunity for my relatives to gently witness to me by their attractive life-styles.

My mother's careful nurture ensured that church-going became part of my Sunday routine. I sang in the choir and became a server in a church in my home town of Crewe. My father died when I was fourteen, and at the age of sixteen I won a county scholarship to attend Atlantic College, an international sixth-form college near Cardiff (where I met my first Muslims from the Arab world). Liberated from the wise restraints of home I spread my teenage wings and discovered the big wide world of the 1960s.

However, the Lord kept me safe; and in the last year the fatherhood of God became personal knowledge to me through faith in Jesus Christ. Cornered by a seemingly impossible human situation, I turned to him in faith. Kneeling in the musty chapel under the shadow of St Donat's Castle I yielded my life to him and experienced the power of the first Pentecost as of a mighty rushing wind.

The only reference point available to me was the Bible. Overnight it became a living book to me. Nothing and nobody could stop my daily devotions, even if it meant hiding away in the music room to read and to pray.

My human situation was turned around. I was offered a place at St John's College Durham to read for a general science degree. Suddenly I was surrounded by Christians who had shared a similar experience and understood what I was talking about, and who wanted to disciple me. I grew fast in this rich fertile soil. I blossomed spiritually and intellectually, and was given responsibilities; first in summer youth camps, and then as the Christian Union Overseas Students Secretary.

It was during this period that I first started praying for missions and witnessing to Muslim students. Also, by this time, I had been accepted by the Church of England for ordination training; and I was going out with a girl who was studying Arabic.

I graduated with an honours degree in anthropology and accepted a place at Clifton Theological College in Bristol. My girlfriend and I decided to spend the summer holiday together on a work project in the Welsh mountains.

One morning while praying in my tent which looked out over a beautiful green hillside, the Lord spoke to me. It was as clear as though he was under the canvas with me. He said, 'You are going to work in the Arab world.' My reply was instantaneous, 'Lord, you must be mad. I don't know anyone in the Arab world.' I was flabbergasted, as I had no intention of going overseas for the Lord. The following summer he confirmed that call, and I worked for two months at the North Africa Mission's Tulloch Memorial Hospital in Tangier, Morocco.

The medical team was headed by Drs Farnham and Janet St John. Their open home was a wonderful testimony to the mainly student team which they hosted every summer. They involved us in as many aspects of the ministry as we were capable of functioning in. For me, that ranged from decorating a hospital ward to preaching in the compound chapel. From that summer on, I always had an interest in the mission; so that later when I joined NAM, I felt as though I was coming home.

During the next year I was a member of the radio team at my theological college. After the merger of three colleges in Bristol we formed a strong team with opportunities to train, and to work with local Radio Bristol which was then in its infancy. I attended the Radio Worldwide radio course at the WEC International centre in Bulstrode where I had my first initiation into missionary radio and the problem of trying to edit a twenty-minute interview to fit a three-minute slot.

The same year God also placed my feet on the soil of another North African country, Tunisia, where I spent nine weeks in Tunis as the locum at the Anglican chaplaincy of St George's. Again I was warmly welcomed by a NAM family who had remained in the capital during the summer. They introduced me to horse meat, though they did not mention this fact until after the very last meal in their home. I met North African believers and had the opportunity to experience another Arab culture at first hand; which further reinforced my call to enter the open door of the Arab world.

I began learning Arabic in my last year at Trinity College (which was the new name of the amalgamated colleges), and wrote an extended essay on 'Christ in the Qur'an' under the guidance of my tutor, Dr J. I. Packer.

At last six years of full-time academic study came to an end. I took up my first curacy in a south Bristol parish of some 20,000 souls under the pastorship of an ex-China Inland Mission missionary and master baker. It was a tough parish with a loving congregation. Together they taught me a lot about ministry. It was a parish which supported the Church Missionary Society; our 'link missionaries' were a family working in Muslim Pakistan who now work in England, and with whom we are still in contact.

This CMS connection got me involved in the local committee, and I was voted on to it as the youth secretary for the area. We arranged a number of joint events for the churches in the region, and missions became a part of my life inside and outside the parish. I married the second summer after being ordained, having made sure on our first date that Janet too had a similar call to the Muslim world.

For a while Morocco passed out of sight. The vicar of the parish left and after an interregnum of three months and an opportunity to work with the new incumbent, we decided that it was time to move. We began knocking on doors and finding out where the Lord wanted us to go next. After talking with several missionary societies we eventually went with CMS to the Middle East. We served with the National Episcopal Church in Cairo, Egypt. Our first goal was to learn colloquial and modern literary Arabic. I ended up by having a variety of responsibilities during the four years we were there. They included being the editor-in-chief of a grass-roots youth magazine in Arabic for the diocese; the acting pastoral provost of the cathedral for an eighteen-month interregnum; the bishop's chaplain; and the cathedral librarian. I even picked up a commission for the BBC's Forces Network, interviewing a once-famous football trainer in Suez.

Our first two children were born in Cairo. By the time we left, we had acquired a considerable amount of experience in living in an Arab culture and had made many wonderful friends, both Egyptian and expatriate.

The Lord opened a new door to us in Amman, Jordan, after the establishment of the new library facility in Cairo. I was invited by the East Jordan Chaplaincy to become their chaplain. The chaplaincy is part of the Arabic episcopal parish of the Church of the Redeemer, a large congregation of mainly Palestinian origin. There had not been a full-time expatriate chaplain for a number of years; but because the foreign English-speaking population of Jordan had grown to meet the economic expansion of the country, there was an urgent need for one. We worked closely in co-operation with the Arabic congregation; my immediate superior was the assistant bishop of the Diocese of Jerusalem. During the four years we served in Jordan I was involved with a variety of ministries, including being on the founding committee of a theological education by extension programme for the Arab world which is now active in at least three countries of the Middle East.

However, Jordan was not to be a long-term assignment, and again the Lord opened a new door to us. The General Director of NAM was making an exploratory trip with his assistant through the Middle East to assess the possibilities of mission expansion. They had been given our name and soon as they landed in Amman we were the first people they looked up. We therefore spent time travelling together around the country and talking about the local situation. Inevitably our own personal circumstances came up, and this lead to prayerful visits to Marseilles and England for interviews.

In due course we were appointed to the mission's media branch in Marseilles, then called the Radio School of the Bible. I became the Director of this unit which was a daunting experience at the beginning because of the nature of the work and the size and international composition of the team. However, I soon realised that the eight years working with nationals and expatriates had prepared me well for the work to which he now opened a new door. Thirteen years had elapsed between the summer I spent in Morocco with NAM and arriving at the RSB in Marseilles, but at each stage the Lord had opened the appropriate doors of ministry.

When NAM changed its name to Arab World Ministries in 1987, three years after our arrival, RSB changed its publicity name to Arab World Media. The primary objective of the centre is Muslim evangelism by means of radio, Bible correspondence courses, and literature. In addition we provide services to the emerging North African church and to the mission. For example, intensive short-term summer Bible schools using TEE

materials written at AW Media have been effectively held
in Spain.

The target audience of our primary ministries is North
African young people between the ages of 18-25. Statistics
published in 1986 put the population of Morocco at 22.4
million with a growth rate of more than half a million per
year. Forty-two per cent of this population were under 15
years of age. These young people are having to face many
challenges as vast numbers join the potential work force
each year; numbers already swollen by the exodus of rural
peoples into the urban conurbations. Islamic fundamen-
talism and communism are the two most attractive
alternatives, and Morocco, Algeria and Tunisia have all
had trials of members of these extremist groups in recent
years.

Disillusioned with their social, political and religious
environment, a growing number from among this mainly
literate urban population are seeking solutions to their
questions. One important means through which they
actively pursue this search is foreign radio broadcasts.
These open windows on the East and West, and on the
reforming and often militant movements of the contemporary Muslim world. Radio is popular, transistor sets are
readily available, and the airwaves are free, private, and
uncensored. 'As I was listening to different radio stations
of the world,' writes one listener, 'I came across a strange
programme that caught my attention, and I listened
attentively . . .' It is very difficult to even make guess-
timations at the numbers listening to Christian broadcasts
in the area, but recent indications are that every evening
there could be five-figure audiences; and over the period
of a year, the number of at least one-time listeners could
be in the order of 100,000. Reports further suggest that
the greatest concentrations of listeners are in cities like
Rabat and Casablanca.

Miss Aicha represents this generation of seekers when
she writes to us, 'My best wishes to *Nour ala Nour* [the
name of our Arabic programme, which means: Light upon

Light]. I am thrilled to hear it in Arabic. You can't imagine how happy we were the day we were able to pick up your programme! We are a group of ten friends, and we have a strong belief in God and our Saviour the Lord Jesus.' Another friend of the programme writes from North Africa, 'Before I wasn't much interested in your programme,' she confesses, 'but the Lord has opened my eyes and my heart, and now I always listen, and the whole family with me. This year I met Christ. I would like to have someone who can help me read the Holy Bible.'

Radio has been the open door which the Holy Spirit has used to plant and nurture churches, but normally it is only the beginning of a long process of bringing people into personal contact with the gospel. There are other vital ministries which complete the chain to a personal commitment to Jesus Christ, to baptism and to integration into a living local fellowship of national believers. At AW Media our first line of follow-up is a comprehensive series of Bible correspondence courses, either written or adapted for people with a Muslim background. Beginning with an introductory course on the whole Bible we follow it with a course on the life of Christ based on St Luke's Gospel and then one on Acts which introduces them to the life of the church. For those who want to go further and deeper there is a series called the 'Five Pillars' and we also use Arabic translations of the Navigators Bible study materials.

All those writing in to the radio programme receive the first lessons of the introductory course, others hear about them from their friends who are already taking the courses, and others still through the literature. But sometimes the Spirit moves in strange and unpredictable ways.

For example, from time to time the North African authorities publish articles in the national Press warning the public to avoid these 'subversive' Christian courses. Along with the article they print a sample of an enrolment coupon. These coupons have been deliberately cut out of the newspaper, completed and forwarded to us by interested students. On another occasion a Moroccan who came to Christ describes how he first came into contact with the courses and through them to Christ: 'Always during Ramadan I died of boredom. One day I was hanging around in the street with a friend. He pulled a green slip of paper from his pocket (the BCC enrolment coupon) and said, "With this paper you can get literature and courses about the Holy Scriptures."'

Literature supplements the biblical knowledge of our BCC students and a thrice-annual magazine called the *Key of Knowledge* appears in Arabic and French. Figures from Algeria demonstrate how a transformation is taking place within North African society at the educational level. After the French left in 1962, Algeria's schools had only 850,000 pupils enrolled. But due to a concerted effort on the part of Algeria's government over the past twenty years, current enrolment stands at 5.4 million. Basic schooling is now compulsory for all children between the ages of 6 and 15, with provision for a further three years of secondary education, for those who desire it. As a result, adult literacy has climbed from 31 per cent in 1962 to 58 per cent in 1986. One effect has been an increase in the number of Arabic and bilingual journals coming on to the book stands. Between 1981 and 1986 the number doubled. This trend is repeated in the other North African countries including Morocco.

When it comes to the challenge this poses the Christian missionary initiative in the Muslim world, one writer bluntly states: 'Muslim scholars have not been sitting idle; they have been building up a great offensive and defensive bulwark in their books to forestall any Christian incursions into Islam.'

The comments of Ali, a Moroccan prisoner, reflect the joy of receiving his copy of the *Key*, 'I have read, admired, and re-read the pages of the Key. I don't take part in your tests to win prizes. The important thing is to know, and not to have. However, I would very much like to have a Bible.' 7,000 copies of the Arabic edition and 5,000 copies of the French are mailed into North Africa and bring the challenge of personal faith in Jesus Christ and the application of the gospel to everyday life just as they did to Ali. Another reader writing in the gracious style of the orient says:

> The 'Key' to true happiness, the efficacious 'Key' for the unenlightened like me. . .in the lines of this paper one can always feel love and faithfulness. I did not believe that such beautiful things could exist in life. The down-to-earth subjects make the 'Key' strong. May all those who work on the newspaper have long life, illuminated by the true light, Jesus Christ.

Radio has been described as 'the missionary who needs no visa', a media by which a Muslim can sit in the privacy of his own home – can even use earphones, if he wishes – and listen to the gospel without fear for his life. But the necessary follow-up ministries very often soon put the contact into a situation of unexpected and uninvited danger. A seventeen-year old girl from a small town in Morocco writes:

> I want to have more information on the subject of the Bible and Jesus Christ. I am lost. I was ignorant of the good life of Jesus. I want to know the truth about God. When I told my friends that I wanted to enroll in your Bible correspondence courses they mocked me. Even my family are not of the same opinion as me.

Kamel was born in Morocco to Muslim parents. They were not 'fanatics' but faithfully observed the fast month of Ramadan like everyone else.

At the age of 16 Kamel's friend handed him a piece of green paper (the BCC coupon). Why not try the lessons? Kamel did. He was captivated by what he read of Moses, Abraham, David and the other prophets. But what impressed him most was the teachings about the Messiah. Yes, he had heard of him before. Islam spoke of him as a prophet, but in these lessons he learned of Jesus as the Saviour from sin. As he reflected on his own religion, he realised it didn't make him acceptable to God. So he decided to place his faith in Jesus and to follow him, to know the assurance of sins forgiven and of being accepted by a Holy God.

Kamel was one day very encouraged to discover that one of his classmates was also a Christian. They talked together about God, faith and Jesus.

Kamel began to realise that he must have more Christian fellowship. He found a small assembly in a neighbouring town and began meeting with the group regularly. He also began sharing his faith with friends and colleagues at work. Colleagues began asking questions. In fact, some even questioned his parents about the Christian meetings. They became embarrassed because of him. Eventually Kamel was called to the police station in his town and questioned:

'Are you a Christian?'

'Yes, sirs.'

'Since when?'

'Since my youth.'

'Who told you about Christianity?'

'A friend shared the Word of God with me.'

'Is he a Christian too?'

'God alone knows that.'

'How did you get the lessons?'

'Very easily; my friend gave me an application form which I sent to the RSB.'

'What was your reaction to the lessons?'

'Very interesting.'

Kamel underwent much questioning; about other Christians in the area, about Christian prayer and about Christian beliefs. He bravely prayed the Lord's Prayer.

'What has *Isa* [the name for Jesus in the Qur'an] done for you?'

'He has given me salvation and eternal life'

'All right, we'll see if your Saviour can deliver you from our hands. If you don't abandon your faith, we'll kill you.'

He was jailed for 96 days in a cell measuring 2×3 metres. 'These days of detention did me a lot of good,' he said.

After his release from prison, Kamel was repeatedly summoned by the police for questioning. His mother advised him to leave the country. All the questionings and threats were too much for her emotions. She bought an airline ticket to France, and Kamel is now studying part-time at a Bible school while waiting for the French authorities' response to his application for nationalisation.

There is a cost in following Jesus Christ in the Muslim world, and Morocco is no exception. But it is a privilege to meet men like Kamel who from time to time pass through Marseilles and visit us and for whom we can pray regularly.

Keith Fraser-Smith

For further information contact:

Arab World Ministries
P.O. Box 51
Loughborough
Leicestershire LE11 0ZQ.

BIBLIOGRAPHY OF BOOKS BY
CHARLES FRASER-SMITH

Charles Fraser-Smith with Gerald McKnight and Sandy Lesberg, *The Secret War of Charles Fraser-Smith: The 'Q' Gadget Wizard of World War Two* (Michael Joseph, 1981). Paperback edition 1983; Second impression 1984; Third printing by Paternoster Press, 1986.

Charles Fraser-Smith with Kevin Logan, *Secret Warriors: Hidden Heroes of MI6, OSS, MI9, SOE and SAS* (Paternoster Press, 1984).

Charles Fraser-Smith, *Men of Faith in the Second World War* (Paternoster Press, 1986).

Charles Fraser-Smith with David Porter, *Four Thousand Year War* (Paternoster Press, 1988).

NOTES

1. Alfred, in later life, became a prominent figure in Crusader work in Watford, and a well-known name in Anglican circles. It was Alfred who, after inviting Charles to speak at a Crusader meeting, informed him afterwards that he thought that his gifts lay elsewhere! The incident played a part in deciding Charles that his missionary work must be primarily practical in nature.
2. The story of General Orde Wingate and the Chindit campaign is told in *Men of Faith*, pp.13–24 (NB: References in these footnotes to Charles's books are by short title. For full details, see the bibliography opposite.
3. See *Four Thousand Year War*, pp.14–141.
4. *Secret Warriors*, p.174.
5. See the chapter on John Laing in *Men of Faith*, pp.113–19.
6. John Laing (who was knighted in 1959) made several such houses available for use by missionaries. 'Houses on several of the estates were set aside for the use of missionaries temporarily in the country on furlough . . . . Beatrice Laing took a close interest in these houses, and ensured provision for the practical needs of their residents' (Roy Coad, *Laing*, Hodder and Stoughton 1979, p.133). Beatrice was Laing's wife.
7. See F.F. Bruce, *In Retrospect* (Pickering and Inglis, 1980), p.115. Bruce recalls that while he was a young man at Leeds University, 'among the civil servants whom we came to know was G. Ritchie Rice, in charge of a department of the MOS; and Charles Fraser-Smith, formerly of Morocco and now of

Bratton Fleming, Devon, was nominally attached to
Mr Rice's department; actually he was engaged on
specially secret and exciting work of 'national
importance'.

8. See *Secret War*, pp.22–23.
9. In 1989 Walter Calvert-Carr remarked in a letter to
   Charles, 'I never cease to admire your enthusiasm and
   tenacity in pursuit of a most worthy cause – a
   twentieth-century crusade!'
10. *Secret War*, p.24.
11. Ibid., p.30.
12. Ian Fleming, *Diamonds Are For Ever* (Jonathan
    Cape, 1965), ch.7.
13. *Secret War*, pp. 127–30; *Secret Warriors*, pp.58, 185.
14. *Secret Warriors*, p.58.
15. The story of the Burma Campaign and Charles's work
    for it is told in *Men of Faith*, ch.3.
16. See *Secret War*, p.100, for further description of this
    radio.
17. See *Secret War*, p.9.
18. G.R. Rumsey, 'Out-doing the Dutch!' *Dairy Farmer*
    (September 1957), pp. 21–23.
19. T.H. Cooper, 'Slatted floors – the next step', *Farmer
    and Stock-Breeder* (18 October 1960), pp. 94–97.
20. Charles Fraser-Smith, 'Eliminations lead to eco-
    nomy', *Dairy Farmer* (October, 1962), pp. 38–39.
21. Charles Fraser-Smith, 'Group buying must be fol-
    lowed by group selling', *Farmer and Stock-Breeder* (4
    April 1961), p.104.
22. Charles Fraser-Smith, 'Economies for dairy farms in
    the 200 acre range', *Farm and Country* (27 February
    1963), pp.210–212, note by the magazine's editor.
23. Ibid.
24. *Four Thousand Year War*, p.152ff.
25. This document is included as an appendix in the
    present book.
26. 'The barons, no doubt, distrusted alike the impartial-
    ity of the pope and the sincerity of the king, but they
    could not distrust the honesty of Stephen Langton
    . . .' (A.L. Poole, *Domesday Book to Magna Carta*,
    Oxford University Press, 2nd edn 1955).

27. See Richard Rutt, Bp of Leicester, *The History of Hand Knitting* (Batsford, 1987), pp. 24, 138, 143, 144–145.
28. Such thinking was characteristic of progressive-minded mission thinking of the period, and stood in sharp contrast to the triumphalist imperialism which had marked some missionary enterprises in the past. The present author, for example, recalls a national student vocation conference at Keele in 1973 when David Bentley-Taylor challenged his hearers to adopt similar future mission strategies to those urged by Darling. At root of the mission approaches of Fraser-Smith, Darling, Bentley-Taylor and many more is a deep concern that indigenous, national Christians should be partners and leaders of Western-initiated missionary enterprise.
29. The NIV has 'fire', and commentators have suggested that 'grass' may refer to flowers. However, even if this reading is valid, it is significant that the AV translators found the image of grass thrown in an oven to be relevant and contemporary.
30. *Four Thousand Year War*, pp. 37–38.
31. Charles Fraser-Smith, 'Saving the Soil', *Crusade* (April 1963), p.14–15.
32. See pp.69–73.
33. The Aylescott Airfield was a particular pleasure to Charles, as Crusader Camps were held there regularly. One boy who attended the Aylescott Camps was Paul Rodman, the son of a Director of British Aerospace. The company was developed from Avro, where Charles had worked for a time when he returned to Britain at the beginning of the war.
34. The information about Arab World Media in this chapter is taken from information supplied by Keith Fraser-Smith and printed in full as Appendix 2 of the present book.

An up-date on AWM

Arab World Ministries is interdenominational and international. Founded in 1881 as The North Africa Mission it
has recently increased from 106 missionaries to over 250.

AWM's objective is to introduce Arab Muslims to the
Christian Gospel and work through discipleship of those
who accept Christ towards the planting of churches
amongst Arabic speaking peoples. Because of the
opposition of Islamic countries to traditional missionary
methods AWM emphasises the importance of radio, Bible
correspondence courses and literature.

Charles Fraser-Smith writes: Broadcasting work is very
costly; but for missionaries to cover this vast area of Islam
would involve hundreds of trained men and women. So
Media Communication is truly an example of missionary
economics and strategy at work.

Islam has long been the most neglected mission field in
the world. Are we now paying for this neglect? To-day
Muslims claim one million adherents world wide and their
religion is spread throughout the world – an advantage
which militant Communism never had. As Communism in
the past threatened the world, so now Islam with its
increasing intolerance is becoming a great danger to world
peace.

There is only one enduring solution – Christ's superb
message of tolerance, love, forgiveness and religious
freedom. Christ lived what He preached. No other has
equalled this record. His life and teaching are unique. He
is the Man of all men.

His greatest command is 'Go into ALL the world and preach the Gospel'. To counteract sin, injustice, evil and false religions and ideologies every Christian, in some way or another, must obey this final command of Christ. There is no greater enterprise on earth than to help spread the Gospel of Christ.

The citadel of Communism is crumbling. Pray that Islam will be the next to succumb.

The royalties from all the books in this series are donated to Arab World Ministries.

In the Autumn of 1990 a new director has been appointed to the AWM Radio HQ in Marseille, and Keith Fraser-Smith has been assigned to AWM Graphics, Worthing, UK, as AWM Media Department Director.